HOMER AND BIBLE

The Origin and Character of East Mediterranean Literature

By

CYRUS H. GORDON

VENTNOR PUBLISHERS
Ventnor, N. J. 08406

PRINTED JANUARY, 1967

VENTNOR PUBLISHERS

Printed in the United States of America

Reprinted by permission from HEBREW UNION COLLEGE ANNUAL,
Volume XXVI, pp. 43-108, 1955

PREFACE TO THE 1967 REPRINTING

When *Homer and Bible* appeared in 1955, it created a stir and evoked extreme reactions pro and con. This was only to be expected because a new development with radical implications had come to light. Since then the subject has grown considerably. I have treated it more comprehensively in *The Common Background of Greek and Hebrew Civilizations* (Norton, New York, 1965); and, as concerns the decipherment of Linear A, quite specifically in *Evidence for the Minoan Language* (Ventnor Publishers, Ventnor, N. J., 1966). Yet *Homer and Bible* remains the best starting place for the student who wishes to be initiated into the subject.

This monograph, now reprinted photomechanically without alteration,[1] marks the creative stage of a subject that is being constantly refined as well as expanded. More detailed and up-to-date contributions have been, and will be, written, but *Homer and Bible* retains its usefulness as the starting point for students embarking on this new and rewarding field of investigation.

Dr. Harry Hoffner, my former student and now my colleague, has taken over my course on *Homer and Bible*. It was he who suggested that this monograph be reissued because he found it more useful for his students than any other publication on this topic. I express my thanks to him as well as to the editors of the *Hebrew Union College Annual*, who have so generously permitted Ventnor Publishers to reprint *Homer and Bible*.

December 2, 1966

Cyrus H. Gordon
Brandeis University
Waltham, Mass. 02154

FOOTNOTE
[1] Of all the corrections that could be made, I limit myself to one. In paragraph 41, "Joab" is an error for "Joab's brother Abishai."

Contents

HOMER AND BIBLE

The Origin and Character of East Mediterranean Literature

CYRUS H. GORDON, Dropsie College

FOREWORD

As early as 1941, I noted that Ugaritic literature is of importance for its connections with Homeric epic (*The Living Past*, New York, 1941, p. 155). Meanwhile the relation between Ugarit and the Bible had become evident from the time the tablets began to be read in the early 'thirties. But it was not until about 1950 that I observed that many of the parallels were triple — Ugaritic, Hebrew and Greek — pointing to an East Mediterranean epic tradition, with roots deep in the second millennium, and underlying Homer and Bible. This tradition keeps reverberating in subsequent literature down to the present day because of the lasting impact of Greece and Israel.

If I say so little about the parallels in Greek historiography and drama, on the one hand, or in rabbinic literature, on the other, it is only because I want at this time to establish the foundations of the subject, rather than to delineate its superstructure. My neglect of the Latin evidence stems from the same cause: Roman culture is an offshoot of the Greek heritage. By the same token, I have resisted the temptation to dwell on postclassical European parallels.

This monograph is compact; perhaps too compact. The reader should refer to the sources cited in any paragraph that interests him. The documentation is adequate but not exhaustive; and many a paragraph in the pages that follow merits the treatment of a whole book. On reading my laconic manuscript I am reminded of the Chinese theological student who, when asked to describe the Book of Hosea, remarked only: "Text corrupt; also women."

For two years now, I have been conducting seminars on the

7

subject of this monograph and discussing the topic with a number of students and friends. Among those who have made constructive comments, I wish to thank Walther Buchholz, Joan K. Gordon, Charles Pfeiffer, Nahum Sarna, Harold Stigers, Elizabeth Thomas, Fred Young and Wilbur Wallis.

CHAPTER I

THE PROBLEM IN BROAD OUTLINE

1. Seas may serve as either barriers or links between groups of mankind. Prior to 1492 the Atlantic separated the people in Europe from those in America. Now, however, it links them ever closer.

2. From the earliest historic times, the Mediterranean linked, rather than separated, the people on its various shores. This monograph deals with the East half of the Mediterranean because the setting in time is relatively early, and in keeping with the general movement of culture from east to west, it was only the East Mediterranean that left written records during the period in question. A glance at the map will show that the distances involved are not great. It is possible to sail from Asia Minor to Crete in short stages coastally and via islands including Rhodes. Moreover, Cyprus lies rather close to Ugarit on the mainland. Even the biggest distances that the East Mediterranean sailor had to cross are tiny compared with those spanned in small craft by Pacific islanders.

3. The existence of an East Mediterranean civilization was made possible by geographic factors.[1] Its hub was Crete, whose

---

[1] By the third millennium the westward movement of Sumero-Akkadian civilization brought it to the shores of the East Mediterranean, and Egyptian culture moved with the Nile into the same area. For people to amount to anything in history, they must be exposed to civilizing forces. But the mere exposure does not guarantee historic greatness. Of the numerous ethnic groups around the East Mediterranean, the Hebrews and Greeks made the most of the challenge and live on as powerful elements in Western Civilization. Others, like the Hittites, Hurrians and Amorites, played considerable roles and disappeared from the scene. Some, like the Moabites, enjoyed a success that was merely local and transitory. Others, like the Perizzites, are only a name. Countless others are not even that.

first cultural remains are prior to the classical Sumerian Era of Mesopotamia and to the Pyramid Age of Egypt in the third millennium. Minoan culture, like every known culture, was indebted to forerunners and outside influences.[2] But its distinctiveness is not inferior to that of Sumer or Old Kingdom Egypt.

4. While the third millennium witnessed the development of the cradles of civilization (notably Sumer, Egypt and Crete), the second millennium produced the international fusion of Near East cultures culminating in the Amarna Age (15th and 14th centuries, B. C.), when the Greeks and Hebrews made their debut on the stage of history.[3]

5. Between about 1750 and 1450, a syllabic script called Linear A[4] was used in Crete. But around the middle of the fifteenth century it gave way to Linear B marking not only a change in the syllabary,[5] but also a change in language. The language of Linear B is Greek; some scholars suggest that we call it the Achaean dialect of Greek. The decipherment of Linear B by Michael Ventris establishes the Greeks as an ethnic factor in the East Mediterranean by the Amarna Age.[6]

6. The Patriarchal Narratives in Genesis are the traditional origins of the Hebrew family. Until the actual personalities and events[7] mentioned in those narratives can be factually linked with extrabiblical sources, the date of the Patriarchal Age will remain subject to disagreement. Meanwhile, two matters are clear: (1) The social institutions reflected in those narratives

[2] C. L. Woolley, *Spadework*, London, 1953, pp. 110–2, discusses interrelations between Crete and the mainland (notably Alalakh, in far north Canaan), stressing the contribution of the mainland to Crete.

[3] For the Amarna date of the Hebrew Patriarchal narratives, see my *Introduction to Old Testament Times*, Ventnor, N. J., 1953, pp. 100 ff.

[4] A. J. Evans, *The Palace of Minos at Knossus* I, 1921, pp. 612–48.

[5] Linear B, however, derived many signs from Linear A; A. J. Evans, *Scripta Minoa* II, Oxford, 1952 (edited by J. L. Myres) lists 69 signs common to A and B (see pp. 6–23 and Table I).

[6] The latest article (at the time of this writing) by M. Ventris is "King Nestor's Four-Handled Cups: Greek Inventories in Minoan Script," *Archaeology* 7, 1954, pp. 15–21. The development of the subject is treated with full documentation by Sterling Dow, "Minoan Writing," *American Journal of Archaeology* 58, 1954, pp. 77–129.

[7] The nine kings named in Gen. 14 are the most hopeful clues.

have their most intimate connections with the legal contracts from Nuzu, and (2) the actual content of those narratives reflects the same standard of what is worthy of saga, that we find in Ugaritic literature. It is worth noting that both the Nuzu and Ugaritic tablets are products of the Amarna Age, suggesting that the Patriarchal Narratives are rooted in the same general period.[8]

7. Since the two primary, pre-Roman elements of Western Civilization are the Greek and Hebrew, it follows that the dawn of Western Civilization is, in a sense, the combination of two branches of East Mediterranean culture that grew in the wake of the Amarna Age. It is herein that the historic significance of our subject lies. However, it is doubtful that the relationship between Greek and Hebrew literatures would have been clear without the evidence of other Near Eastern texts, especially those from Ugarit, which (more than any other) serve as the connecting link between Homer and the Bible.

8. The spirits pervading Greek and Hebrew literatures are quite different from each other. Indeed the normal difference between any two nations in an international complex can alter drastically the manifestations of their common heritage. The historic connections between Israel and Mesopotamia[9] are established beyond question; but could any cultures be less similar than the Hebrew and Assyrian? No scholar denies the intimate relations between Ugarit and the Bible, and yet the atmospheres of the two are worlds apart. Nor must we reckon only with national differences, for personal differences can be enormous. Homer and Hesiod are the two leading names in Greek epic, but in spite of the same language and meter, it would be hard to conceive of two poems less alike than the *Iliad* and *Works and Days.* Ezekiel and Deutero-Isaiah are Hebrew prophets not

---

[8] The most recent discussion is my "The Patriarchal Narratives," *Journal of Near Eastern Studies* 13, 1954, pp. 56–59.

[9] As examples we may note: (1) Genesis derives Abraham from Ur via Haran. (2) The Hebrew and Mesopotamian deluge stories are intimately related in detail. (3) Mesopotamian merchants introduced their law as the norm for writing contracts in Canaan. Thus, at Ugarit, the contracts are normally written in Babylonian.

separated so much in time and place; yet their divergent personalities have imparted radically different spirits to their respective books. Relationships, therefore, are not disproved by differences, any more than they are proved by accidental or sparse similarities.

9. By the time an international heritage filters through different national milieus and is then reshaped by individual authors, the various reflexes of that international heritage may be so transformed that the average observer will fail to see the common denominator. This has happened to Hebrew and Greek literatures, regarded by their devotees as "the miracle of Zion" or "the miracle of Athens" respectively; whereas actually the literatures (and for that matter the entire civilizations) of the Greeks and Hebrews are parallel structures built upon the same East Mediterranean foundation.

10. Evidence in historic studies should be as diversified as possible. This monograph is the philological counterpart of fully established archeological conclusions. The Minoan[10] impact on Greece is so well known as to be banal. The Minoan evidence in Egypt and on the entire Syro-Palestinian coast is familiar to every East Mediterranean archeologist who has dealt with the comparative problems of the area. Moreover, the bearing of this (including the new material from Ugarit) on the Homeric problem has not escaped the attention of authors like H. L. Lorimer, *Homer and the Monuments* (London, 1950). Yet it is odd that even Lorimer uses only archeological material from Ugarit without a single reference to any Ugaritic epic passage. It stands to reason that, if Ugaritic artifacts have some bearing on Homeric epic, Ugaritic epic should have an even closer bearing thereon. Material should be compared primarily with like material: archeological with archeological, literary with literary. But this has not been done except for a scrap here and a scrap there.[11]

---

[10] *E. g.*, R. Hamann, *Griechische Kunst*, Munich, 1949, pp. 35–56, where Minoan and Mycenean art is the backdrop for the subsequent periods of Greek art.

[11] The best discussion of the pre-Ugaritological parallels is W. Baumgartner, "Israelitisch-griechische Sagenbeziehungen," *Schweiz. Archiv f. Volkskunde* 41, 1944, pp. 1–29.

11. Along with the diversity of evidence (linguistic, philological, artistic, archeological, sociological, etc.), it is necessary to establish contacts in time and place, if parallels are to stand as organic. In Egypt of the Eighteenth Dynasty, Cretans bearing Cretan gifts are depicted on murals. In the Twentieth Dynasty, Ramses III had to rescue Egypt by warding off an invasion of Mediterranean folk, including Minoanized Greeks such as the Philistines. Meanwhile, Ugarit had a Minoan colony which ties in with the Minoan art objects found there, and with the presence of a Caphtorian god of arts-and-crafts in the Ugaritic pantheon.[12] The distinctiveness of the Phoenicians, vis-à-vis the kindred Semites of the Syrian hinterland, observable in art and seamanship, must be due in large measure to the impact of East Mediterranean (notably Minoan) folk who reached Phoenicia by ship, during the second millennium. R. A. S. Macalister[13] was right in pointing this out, along with the decisive Philistine influence in shaping the civilization of Biblical Palestine.[14] In the Patriarchal Period, the Philistines are peaceful folk around Gerar and Beersheba. Later came fresh invasions of more definitely Greek and warlike Philistines (around the time of Ramses III, and centering about the Pentapolis), who subjugated the Hebrews from the period of the Judges until the victories of David. The rise of the Hebrews from obscurity and tribalism to nationhood and empire, was their response to the Philistine stimulus. The Philistines, who had migrated from the heart of the East Mediterranean, were the chief cultural influence brought to bear on Israel, during the latter's formative period. The leadership of the Achaeans in the Iliad hails from the Mycenean centers of the Peloponnesus; and their allies include a sizable contingent from

[12] For the pre-Ugaritological evidence, see E. Meyer, *Geschichte des Altertums*, 2nd ed., Stuttgart and Berlin, II, 1, 1928, pp. 162–220. All the Ugaritic sources can be located quickly in the Glossary of my *Ugaritic Manual*, Rome, 1955.

[13] *The Philistines: Their History and Civilization*, London, 1914.

[14] What happened is reflected in the name "Palestine"="Philistia." And yet we must repeat that cultural influences between Canaan and Crete were not one-way affairs. Thus Phoenician influence on Crete may be reflected in Il. 14:321–2 where Zeus speaks of "the daughter of far-famed Phoenix that bore me Minos."

Crete itself. Accordingly the conclusions of this monograph would (even if we lacked the evidence at our disposal and presented in the following pages) have been a justifiable inference for the East Mediterranean in the wake of the Amarna Age.[15]

12. East Mediterranean literature can be expected in any island or coastal country in the entire area during the centuries in question. Its representatives are now available from Egypt (Late Egyptian Stories),[16] Canaan (Ugarit[17] and Hebrew), Anatolia (Hittite literature[18] and historiography), and Greece (starting with Homer and Hesiod). It is at present impossible to make extensive use of the Linear B material because all of the texts therein are economic and administrative. But it is only a matter of time before Minoan literary texts will be discovered on clay tablets. The influence of Babylonian writing habits was too strong during the Amarna Age to have left no literary texts in the East Mediterranean. It took until 1929 to discover them in Canaan (at Ugarit). Meanwhile, let us not forget that only a fraction of the many cities of Crete[19] have been excavated.

13. It will occur to some readers that Higher Criticism of the Bible and Homer should receive more attention than it gets in this study. However, it is well to remember that Higher Criticism is a legacy from a period before the age of archeological and epigraphical discovery. The impact of the age of discovery has not yet been adequately felt in philological circles, partly due to the deep roots of philological tradition, and partly due to the departmentalization that often segregates philologian from

---

[15] This general date refers to the period depicted in early Greek and Hebrew literatures; and not to the later periods, when our documents were redacted in their present form. The Amarna Age antiquity of much Greek and Hebrew material is demonstrated by the Ugaritic parallels pointed out in the following pages.

[16] See G. Lefebvre, *Romans et contes égyptiens de l'époque pharaonique*, Paris, 1949.

[17] See my *Ugaritic Literature*, Rome, 1949.

[18] *Cf.* A. Lesky, "Hethitische Texte und griechischer Mythos," *Anzeiger der phil.-hist. Klasse der Österreichischen Akademie der Wissenschaften* 1950, no. 9, pp. 137–59.

[19] Od. 19:174 refers to the 90 cities of Crete. However schematic this number may be, it is interesting as a parallel to the 90 cities captured by Baal (Ug. 51:VII:12).

archeologist. No one in his right mind will deny that compositions such as the Iliad or Genesis are what the word "composition" implies. Like all creations, they are not fashioned *ex nihilo*.
A masterpiece such as the Iliad can only be the culmination of a
long and rich tradition. Its author fell heir to a large repertoire
of epic material, from which he could select, to which he could
add, and which he could modify so as to create a finished masterpiece that remains unexcelled in world epic. To detach this episode or that document[20] and ascribe an early or a late date is
an arbitrary procedure that will not enlighten us at a time
when we can more profitably restudy the classics against the
background of newly discovered sources.

14. The "P" stratum of the Pentateuch is generally ascribed
to the period of the Second Temple (say, the Fifth Century,
B. C.). However, newly discovered texts show that much of the
material ascribed to P is very early, even pre-Mosaic.[21] Accordingly, the distinguished and deviationist Higher Critic, Ezekiel
Kaufmann, makes P the earliest instead of the latest stratum in
the Pentateuch, or at least pre-D. The designation of attributing
hypothetical dates to hypothetical strata, as "historical"[22] is
a misnomer that need not deceive us. Whether one builds a
system on Wellhausen's "orthodox" Higher Criticism or on
Kaufmann's "heretical" Higher Criticism, makes little difference
methodologically. In this monograph there is no desire to con-

[20] W. J. Woodhouse, *The Composition of Homer's Odyssey*, Oxford, 1930,
carries on the tradition of T. W. Allen, *Homer: The Origin and the Transmission*,
Oxford, 1924, in attacking the conventional Higher Criticism of Homer. What
Woodhouse (p. 240) says about Homer's expressions holds *mutatis mutandis*
for the content of Homer at other levels as well: "The words and phrases and
turns of expression . . . have been used a thousand times yet with each re-
petition the poet hits the nail on the head, and his lines seem newly minted
for just this place and occasion."

[21] Cases in point are the elements of the flood story that go back to old
Mesopotamian origins; *e. g.*, the reeds (Hebrew *qānîm*, not *qinnîm*) in Gen.
6.14 telling of the construction of the ark (*cf. Introduction to Old Testament
Times*, p. 38, n. 31).

[22] O. Eissfeldt ("Recht und Grenze archäologischer Betrachtung des Alten
Testaments," *Orientalistische Literaturzeitung* 49, 1954, pp. 101–8), while
defending "die historisch-kritische Wissenschaft" (p. 108), admits the need of
revising it in view of the growing corpus of facts.

struct a system, but only to go where the facts in the sources lead us.

15. Colophons on the literary tablets from Ugarit date them in the reign of King Niqmad II, who paid tribute to the Hittite monarch Suppiluliuma, thus providing us with a *terminus ad quem* in the fourteenth century B. C. So, if there is a clear parallel of an organic character between Ugaritic literature, on the one hand, and Hebrew or Greek literatures, on the other, the element involved must be pre-Mosaic and pre-Homeric, and not as late as the conventional date ascribed to the Biblical or Homeric stratum by pre-1929 scholarship.[23] For example, H. T. Wade-Gery, (*The Poet of the Iliad*, Cambridge, 1952, pp. 32 ff.), committing himself to the "hypothesis" that Homer "was a considerable innovator" (p. 32), cites as an example of Homer's originality, Iliad 1:198 ff. (p. 41) about Athena's intervention in a quarrel, when Achilles draws his sword on Agamemnon. However, as we shall note below (§157), the scene is pre-Homeric and now attested in Ugarit.

16. The hypercritical approach to Homeric or Biblical problems persists among so many professional scholars that some authors find it worthwhile to combat it. There are many reputable Bible scholars who maintain that references to the Philistines in the Patriarchal Narratives are anachronistic. That the establishment of the Philistines (*qua* Caphtorians[24]) in Palestine since pre-Patriarchal times is indicated by all the pertinent evidence[25] has still not eradicated the fallacious hypercritical view. Similarly V. Bérard devoted much of his career to authenticating the Phoenician contacts in the Homeric poems,[26] even though there was never any real reason to doubt the authenticity

---

[23] This refers not only to works written before the discovery of the Ugaritic tablets in 1929, but also to subsequent books that have not recognized the bearing of the tablets on the problem.

[24] "Philistine" overlaps and even interchanges with "Cretan" (Ezek. 25.16) or "Caphtorian" (Deut. 2.23; Amos 9.7; etc.).

[25] *Introduction to Old Testament Times*, pp. 108–9.

[26] See especially *Les Phéniciens et l'Odyssée* I–II, Paris, 1927. Other books of Bérard that may interest the reader, include *La résurrection d'Homère: Le drame épique*, Paris, 1930; *L'Odyssée d'Homère*, Paris, 1931; and *Tables Odysséennes*, Paris, 1932 (with Greek-Semitic vocabulary).

of Phoenicia in the world of either the Iliad or Odyssey, no matter how early a date one might choose from all the dates ever proposed for either poem. And yet L. A. Stella has, not without good reason, deemed it necessary to demonstrate that the Phoenicians are attested in the second millennium at Ugarit, so that they cannot be considered anachronistic in Homer; see her article "Importanza degli scavi di Ras Shamra per il problema fenicio dei poemi omerici," *Archeologia Classica* 4, 1952, pp. 72–76.

17. The surest clue to the outside influence on any literature comes from the literature itself. If the reader wants a factual key to what the Homeric epics owe to the East Mediterranean, all he has to do is to scan the geographical names in an indexed edition of Homer. There he will find that Egypt, Phoenicia, Syria, the whole coast of Asia Minor, Crete, Cyprus and other islands are in the Homeric world. If one looks at the proper names in the Ugaritic tablets, he will find Caphtor (=Crete and nearby areas), Alashia (=Cyprus), Lebanon, Sidon, Tyre, Syria, Edom, the Hittites and Egypt among them. If one reads the Bible with regard for the foreign names, he will see that Ionia,[27] the Hittites, Crete,[28] Cyprus,[29] Philistia, Edom and Egypt are among them. Moreover, it is instructive to note in what contexts, periods and with what frequency such names occur. Egyptian references to the Mediterranean, especially around the Syro-Palestinian coast, abound in Egyptian records. Thus each literature tells us where to look for the interrelations in any given period and in what branch of cultural activity. A study of the Homeric, Ugaritic, Phoenician, Hebrew, Egyptian, Minoan, Anatolian and other East Mediterranean onomastica will point to the same conclusions as the present study of the literary texts.

18. More evidence is bound to come up. The day may arrive when the combined bulk of Anatolian, Minoan, Ugaritic and Egyptian literary texts may rival that of Hebrew, if not of Greek. With more evidence we shall be able to check our results in

---

[27] Hebrew *Yāwān*.

[28] Called "Caphtor."

[29] Hebrew *Kittîm* refers to the Cypriotes of Kition, if not of the whole island.

detail and refine our conclusions. But at any given time, we can only use what we actually possess. Nor will the day ever come when we shall be certain that no more evidence will come to light. The broad outlines of East Mediterranean literary developments are now clear. Moreover, the crucial evidence from Ugarit has not hitherto been brought to bear on this question which lies at the heart of the origins of Western Civilization. This alone calls for the exposition of the subject at this time.

19. Method comes out of the problem and its material. It was natural enough for the Homeric problem to be tackled in terms of fine-art, weapons, metals, etc. when archeological evidence from Troy, Mycenae, Knossos and other sites evoked a re-evaluation. This monograph deals with the bearing of new literary evidence on old literary classics. Some of the parallels are due to simple references to widespread institutions or materials. Others are more narrowly literary, being of a stylistic character. The mass of the evidence, however, is actual narrative content, reflecting what people in the East Mediterranean considered worthy of saga. That certain elements are taken from daily life, while others are fantastic, makes little difference for present purposes. That the wondrous use of the Greek aegis is exactly the same as the Hebrew "staff of God" (§126) may at first seem more impressive than the parallels concerning real life. But this should not be so upon deeper reflection. To clarify this, we may point out that personal beauty (§85) and sex scandal (§§86–92) occur in all societies and periods. Yet both phenomena occur *frequently* in the Hebrew historical books (Genesis through Kings) down through David's reign and *never* thereafter. What is worthy of saga transcends the unimaginative distinction between reality and fancy.

20. A distinguished classicist, in noting the economic character of the Linear B tablets, despairs of finding an "Ur-Ilias" in the Minoan sphere.[30] As I see it, however, the Ur-Ilias of Crete has already been found, albeit in Semitic dress. The Ugaritic Legend of Kret is of Cretan derivation as the name of the hero indicates. Like the Iliad, the story concerns a war waged so

---

[30] S. Dow, *American Journal of Archaeology* 58, 1954, pp. 77–129.

that a king might regain his rightful wife who is being withheld from him, in a distant city. This theme is found nowhere among known texts in any language prior to our East Mediterranean tablets of the Amarna Age. It is alien to the older extant literatures of Egypt and Mesopotamia. That it permeated the East Mediterranean is clear from the fact that it occurs in truncated form also in the Bible, which tells us that David won the Princess Michal as wife, but that she was taken away from him so that he had to rewin her later. David's career was intertwined with Philistine contacts. Hence in time and place, we expect his saga to bear the stamp of East Mediterranean tradition. Royal epic in the East Mediterranean tradition called for the theme of the king losing his bride and then rewinning her.[31]

21. The people of the East Mediterranean (with the exception of Egypt) tended to be split up into little districts or tribes. Israel has left a record of how it emerged from tribalism to nationhood, only to split again into two kingdoms upon the death of Solomon. But the aim of reuniting all the tribes remained the ideal of the prophets and political leaders of stature.[32] The Greeks were not united before Alexander, and upon his death they split into a number of kingdoms. Leaders of nations like Israel and Greece had the problem of welding disparate elements into a unified whole. This characterized not only the two most important people of the East Mediterranean as seen from our vantage point (to wit, Israel and Greece)[33] but others as well. Indeed there could be no nation in the entire area (outside Egypt) without a vigorous and conscious process of ethnic integration.

22. The traditions of early Israel aim at establishing a feeling of kinship and common destiny of a group of ethnic elements idealized as The Twelve Tribes. To accomplish this, the latter are made the descendants of one and the same Patriarch. They

---

[31] The romantic elements in the Mahâbhârata and Râmâyana suggest that Indo-Europeans injected this mood into East Mediterranean epic.

[32] This holds for the north (Hos. 2.2) as well as south; and for the pre-Exilic (Jer. 3.18; 33.7; 50.4), Exilic (Ezek. 37.15–22; 47.13) and post-Exilic (Zech. 8.13) prophets.

[33] Importance is here measured by effect on subsequent history.

are further bound by a common history in which wars by, and even among, the tribes are portrayed without condemning or embittering any of the tribes, but rather depicting them as kinsmen destined for nationhood together. Moreover, the narratives are calculated to excite interest in their warlike ancestors rather than to alienate tribe from tribe.[34] The culmination of Israel's heroic age (§90) is the Monarchy united and glorious under David. The Law, or Five Books of Moses, have for millennia been the core of Hebrew tradition, for while they do not tell of the Conquest and Davidic Monarchy, they establish the kinship of the tribes, their common religion and law, their emergence as a people in the Exodus, and their arrival at the Promised Land with the divine assurance of possessing it.[35] The use to which the Law was put appears in the account of the reign of Josiah (II Kings 22–23). The King wanted to reunite Israel and Judah. The discovery of the Law in 621 B. C. during his reign and his summoning of the people to Jerusalem for a seven day celebration of the Passover, were leading features of his program. The Passover (rather than the other pilgrimage festivals: Pentacost and Tabernacles) became the national festival par excellence because it celebrates the Exodus when all the tribes emerged from obscurity to nationhood. During Passover the entire Law could be read to the people. A Passover convocation was much like a Greek panegyris; the entire Pentateuch could be read at the one, much as the entire Iliad might be read at the other.[36] Since the 5,845 verses of the Law number but a fraction of the 16,673 lines of the Iliad, which was read *in toto* at convocations such as the Great Panathenaia in Athens, I cannot subscribe to the prevailing view that Josiah's Law book must have been only a part of Deuteronomy. Rather must it have been much

[34] Note how II Sam. 1 depicts interdynastic respect; the Judean David expresses admiration and love for the Benjaminite dynasty that he supplanted.

[35] Indeed the omission of subsequent history with its fatal divisions, would favor the reconciliation of Israel and Judah. In this regard, the position of the Samaritans (whose Canon is limited to the Pentateuch) had something in its favor.

[36] The Samaritans read from the Pentateuch before the sacrifice of the paschal lamb.

like our present Pentateuch, including certainly the Patriarchal narratives and the Exodus which are indispensable for fulfilling the main purpose of convocations such as Josiah's; namely, national union.

23. We are to view the Iliad in the same light. As a whole, it is a literary masterpiece; but its purpose was not art for art's sake. Nor are we to be deceived by its introduction into thinking that the *raison d'être* of that epic is the wrath of Achilles. The aim of the Iliad is to provide the far-flung members of the Greek people with an epic that would help weld them into a great nation. The ideal of the Iliad was not accomplished until Alexander's reign. But in the meantime the Iliad had paved the way for Alexander's achievement. If we examine the Iliad in this light, what do we find? First, it does not divide Greek from Greek. The Trojans and their allies are treated with as much decorum and honor as the Achaeans and their allies. Moreover, in the Catalogue of the Ships and in scattered descriptions of heroes (on both sides) with their genealogies, satisfaction is given to all the elements of the Hellenic world: in Greece, Asia Minor and the islands. Pilgrims from widely scattered areas, attending the festivals where the Iliad was read, could listen with pride to the glories of their own epic hero, no matter whether they were Ionian, Cretan, or Peloponnesian. The Iliad tells how once the Greek world had participated in the glorious and manly Trojan War; listening to the Iliad could only inspire the entire Greek people with heroic sentiments and the vision of nationhood.

24. Nor was it necessary for a national program to be aimed at an ethnic unity, such as the Greek or Hebrew. (Besides nations like Italy, France and Germany, there can exist also a Switzerland, whose varied elements are firmly united). The little realm of Ugarit was full of different ethnic groups: Hurrian, Hittite, Subarean, Cypriote, etc. There is a ritual text (no. 2) to be read aloud at public convocations for the purpose of uniting them all into the Ugaritic body politic.

25. Thus Israel, Greece and Ugarit had texts for the great problem in that part of the world: national union. The texts of each nation differ enormously from each other. Ugaritic text 2 is a ritual cementing the component ethnic elements of the realm through its leaders. The Iliad extols the heroism of the far-flung Greek world to inculcate unity; and this is couched in matchless artistry. The Pentateuch is far more complex than either its little Ugaritic or majestic Greek counterpart. It is infinitely more many-sided than any other national epic of any age. But perhaps its most distinctive feature is its universal framework. Genesis leads up to the Patriarchs with the story of the Creation and the peoples of the world, showing how Israel fits into the broad scheme of things. The Bible and the Iliad are parallel responses to the same East Mediterranean stimulus that evoked literary instruments for shaping nations throughout the area. While it is true that Hebrew and Greek authors made the Bible and Iliad, it is also conversely true that the Bible and Iliad made the Hebrew and Greek nations.[37]

26. The Odyssey too has a prehistory enshrined in the literature of the ancient Near East. It has not escaped the notice of orientalists that the Odyssey, insofar as it is the episodic wanderings of a hero, is anticipated by the Gilgamesh Epic. However, there are major differences between the two. Thus while the Odyssey unfolds on the sea and its shores, Gilgamesh's peregrinations are (with one exception) continental.[38] This is not to deny that the Gilgamesh Epic, which enjoyed enormous popularity in the ancient Near East and was widely translated into foreign languages including Hittite (which came into contact with Ionia), has had some ultimate effect on Homer's Odyssey.[39] But there is a much more intimate parallel: the Egyptian Odyssey of Wenamon in the eleventh century B. C.[40] Wenamon was sent

[37] It is instructive to note that the keen devotion of the modern Israelis to the Bible is nationalistic rather than religious.

[38] The continental wanderings of the Hebrew Patriarchs (to and from Mesopotamia, Canaan and Egypt) may be due in part to literary motifs requiring such peregrinations that terminate in homecoming. However, while the Gilgamesh Epic, Sinuhe, Shipwrecked Sailor, Wenamon and Odyssey deal with the homecoming of a wandering individual, the climax of the Patriarchal wanderings is the homecoming of a nation.

[39] Since we possess parts of the Gilgamesh Epic in Hittite translation, it is quite probable that the story reached the Greeks on the Ionian coast before the traditional date of the Trojan War.

[40] The most convenient reference book for many of the oriental compositions discussed in this monograph is J. B. Pritchard, *Ancient Near Eastern*

on a mission to Byblos. Like Odysseus, he traveled by ship on the East Mediterranean. En route, he had misadventures and escapades at Dor, just south of Haifa. After fulfilling his mission (and for that matter, even before fulfilling it), he wants to go home to Egypt. Pursued by enemies, he is forced to sail to Cyprus, where he seeks protection from the Island Queen. There the papyrus breaks off, and we have no more of the story, except the clear inference that he at last got home again. Wenamon and the Odyssey are both episodic wanderings of a guileful hero, from isle to isle and shore to shore in the East Mediterranean. Many an episode is a narrow escape from a tight squeeze. The unifying thread is the goal of coming home after long years of wandering.

27. The question arises as to whether the general character of Wenamon's story is a product of Egypt. There is actually every reason to answer in the affirmative. Late Egyptian literature (including Wenamon) had behind it the world's first secular literature; namely, the Middle Egyptian Stories. The most famous of the latter is the Romance of Sinuhe, according to which the hero Sinuhe, after many years of wandering and sojourning in Syria, at last reaches his goal of coming home again to Egypt. Thus Middle Kingdom Egypt already had the story of homecoming after long years of absence and wandering *on land*. But there is another Middle Egyptian story called the Shipwrecked Sailor, telling how an Egyptian was shipwrecked on a magic isle, and, only after harrowing experiences, is rescued and returns home laden with gifts by the huge serpent inhabiting the isle. The sea of that tale is the Red Sea. The wreck of Odysseus on wondrous isles is a parallel that has been noted by scholars.[41] We could add further analogues in detail, such as Odysseus' coming home laden with the gifts of the Phaeacians, who dwelt on a wondrous isle. But the important consideration is that Middle Egyptian stories attest the motifs of episodic wandering (in Sinuhe) and of hazardous adventure by sea (in Shipwrecked Sailor) — both culminating in homecoming — which

Texts (Relating to the Old Testament), Princeton, 1950. See pp. 25–29 for J. Wilson's translation of Wenamon with bibliography for the sources.

[41] Lefebvre, *op. cit.*, discusses such comparative studies.

were combined in Wenamon with a shift of scene to the East Mediterranean: the hub of international civilization from the Amarna Age on. The Odyssey is the Greek masterpiece of the same East Mediterranean theme going back to Egyptian origins.

28. The Odyssey has no momentous problem. It is a first-rate story; the interest is narrative, however high its dactylic hexameters rank in the annals of world poetry. In Western literature it is the first (and, in poetry, still the best) composition designed for entertainment; and in this it is eminently successful. No matter how much the Odyssey surpasses Egyptian entertainment literature, it owes its essential entertaining nature to its Egyptian forerunners with roots in extant Middle Egyptian stories. Thus, Occidental pleasure literature is a development, through the Odyssey, of a well-documented Egyptian contribution. Why it was Egypt that made this contribution is clear. The nations of the Near East had to struggle constantly with the urgent problem of nationhood; first, to create nations out of ethnic fragments by building a feeling of kinship, solidarity and the morale to fight for land; then, to hold on to what was won. The latter necessity never ended until the destruction of the nation. The one exception to this pattern in the area was Egypt, which by around 3000 B. C. had evolved a homogeneous civilization throughout Upper and Lower Egypt. Egypt had little to fear from the outside; the land was approachable only from the north and south extremities of the long Nile valley. Egyptian nationhood was a firm reality that needed no propaganda or epic. Egypt at times conquered foreign areas, but was not itself invaded except for the relatively brief Hyksos interlude, until the seventh century B. C. When Middle Egyptian entertainment literature was created, Egypt had never been invaded. Accordingly, Egypt was the one nation of Near East antiquity so released from the burden of nationalism that it could produce the light literature[42] which reached Europe via the Odyssey.

29. We have seen (§§ 23, 25, 26) that the Iliad and Odyssey,

---

[42] All nations have diverting tales in oral form. But the Egyptians went on to transform such tales into a written literature because of their earthly conception of the afterlife, which required good reading among the pleasures of the deceased. Our copies of Sinuhe, for example, come from burials.

each viewed as a whole, follow plots that were also in vogue along the Syrian and Egyptian shores of the Mediterranean. Much of the discussion in the ensuing chapters will deal with isolated incidents and details. That we are dealing with genetic relationships, rather than accidental parallels, follows from the fact that both as whole entities and, at the same time, in innumerable details, there is demonstrable agreement. No comparable array of parallels can be made between Homeric Epic and the pre-Amarna literatures of Egypt and Mesopotamia. Our conclusions are precisely what is indicated by considerations of time, place and historic developments.

30. It cannot be stated too emphatically that our literary evidence is supported by every other kind of available evidence, without any contradiction. Because there is full agreement on the part of all competent archeologists, there is no point in rehashing long-known archeological evidence (though we shall indicate new archeological data from time to time below). Yet it is worth pointing out some linguistic evidence in the international vocabulary of the ancient East Mediterranean.

31. Homeric *dorp-* (Il. 19:208) "food, a meal," has no plausible Indo-Hittite etymology. It is identical with Egyptian *drp*, "to feed, offer food to." Since *drp* is attested in Old Egyptian of the third millennium,[43] it appears that it moved from Egypt toward Greece, via the Mediterranean.

32. Hebrew *mᵉk̄ērā(h)* (Gen. 49.5) has long been identified with Greek *mak̄aira*, "sword." It is no wonder that the warlike Philistines taught the Hebrews such a military term.[44]

33. Since the Philistines hailed from the Caphtorian seat of a great architectural tradition,[45] it was natural for them to intro-

[43] The form of the Pyramid Texts is *dꜣp*.

[44] The Philistines were more than just fighters; they had a technology that supplied their troops with armament and they pursued a policy that kept Israel disarmed and without the technology for making or maintaining weapons (I Sam. 13.19–23). It has long been agreed that the Hebrews borrowed the military term *ḳôbaʿ*, "helmet," from the Philistines.

[45] This is abundantly evident in the actual buildings excavated at East Mediterranean sites of the second millennium B. C. in Canaan and Asia Minor. At Ugarit the architectural finds dovetail with the texts that depict the deity who erects temples as a native of Caphtor (§§141–2).

24

duce a word for "chamber"; to wit, Heb. *liškā(h)* (cf. Greek *leskê*, which has no Semitic etymology).[46]

34. The technically superior Philistines apparently introduced new kinds of torches and lamps, to judge from the non-Semitic loanword *lappîd* in early Hebrew;[47] cf. Greek *lampades*. The name of Deborah's husband, Lappidoth, confirms the borrowing during the Heroic Age.

35. The Kret text records, as worthy of saga, the baking of large bread supplies to equip a large troop movement.[48] This explains the emphasis on the baking of *maṣṣā(h)*, a non-Semitic word meaning "unleavened bread," in the account of the Exodus from Egypt. The related Greek *maza*, "barley cake," points to a loan into Hebrew via the Philistines, who may have introduced the Cretan custom as attested in the Cretan Epic of Kret. It is interesting to note that a military institution of the warlike Philistines has been transformed into a cultic phenomenon of Judaism.

36. Another non-Semitic Hebrew word of cultic importance is *mûm*, "blemish," which can hardly be dissociated from Greek *môm(os)*, "blame." Hebrew ritual purity required that sacrificial animals be "without blemish." This expression may reflect East Mediterranean values that transcended cultic usage, for in Homer *amymôn* "without blemish," is frequently applied to heroes and heroines.

37. The important field of Minoan loanwords in Egyptian and Northwest Semitic[49] is about to unfold because of the incipient decipherment of the Linear B tablets. The controls at our disposal from the Egyptian and Semitic ends are fortunately good. In brief, they are as follows: A cultural term that appears in Egyptian during the second millennium, but is absent in Old Egyptian,[50] merits investigation as a Minoan loan. The same

[46] As noted by E. Renan (see A. J. Evans, *Scripta Minoa* I, Oxford, 1909, p. 77, n. 3).

[47] As noted by Sayce (see Evans, *loc. cit.*).

[48] Krt:83 ff., 174 ff.

[49] This covers Canaanite (Hebrew, Phoenician and closely kindred dialects), Ugaritic and Syro-Aramaic.

[50] I. e., of the Pyramid Age in the third millennium,

holds for non-Semitic words, absent in East[51] and South[52] Semitic, but appearing in Northwest Semitic upon contact with the Minoans in the second millennium. If one and the same word (such as *hdm* or *tkt* in §§38, 39) occurs in both Egyptian and Northwest Semitic under the conditions stated above, the Minoan derivation becomes highly probable, since continental African derivation is unlikely for Northwest Semitic, and continental Asiatic derivation is unlikely for Egyptian. Substantiation rests with the forthcoming evidence from Linear B. (But we must realize that Mediterranean vocabulary, even if attested in Linear B, may come from a host of origins.)

38. *Hᵃdōm*, "footstool," is attested only in Northwest Semitic (Ugaritic, Hebrew, Syriac) and Egyptian after the impact of Minoan influence (§37). The Ugaritic god of craftsmanship fashions *hdm id* (51:I:35) " a footstool of Ida"=an Idaean or Cretan footstool. (Note Il. 14:240 for Hephaistus as fashioner of thrones with footstools.) It is natural that the Minoans should leave lexical evidence of their exports; cf. the artistic creations called *kaftôrîm* in Hebrew, named after Caphtor. Ida, the high mountain in central Crete, was associated in antiquity with artistic workmanship.[53] The name "Ida" may be the clue to the source of major elements in the Hebrew creation account, which are not of Egyptian or Mesopotamian origin. Gen. 2.6 states that " *'ēd* rises out of the earth and waters all the surface of the ground." The traditional rendering of *'ēd* as "mist" and the pan-Babylonian identification with Sumerian *id* "river" are unsatisfactory. Rivers do not rise; they descend. What rises from the earth to water the ground is a mountain carrying its streams to the surrounding countryside. Accordingly, it is worth considering that *'ēd* means Ida, pointing to East Mediterranean elements in the Biblical Creation. (There is one objection, however, that requires clarification; namely, that the Greek form of Ida begins with long *î-*, whereas *'ēd* reflects short *i-*. Finesse

---

[51] *Viz.*, Akkadian with its Babylonian and Assyrian dialects.

[52] To wit, Arabic, South Arabic and Ethiopic.

[53] Pliny (Natural History 7:56, 197) reports that Hesiod stated that the Idaean Dactyls taught the smelting and tempering of iron in Crete (§141).

in the phonetics of East Mediterranean loans will take some time to establish.)

39. There is a kind of ship called _ṭkt_ in Ugaritic and _skty_ in Egyptian.[54] The appearance of this word in time and in place, as well as other circumstances as outlined in §37, point to Minoan origin. The meaning is appropriate for a loan introduced by the seafaring Minoans. Since some of the Linear B tablets concern ships, we may expect further data from Crete in the near future.

40. It is inevitable that the subject of our investigation will eventually put Greek and Hebrew culture in lights quite different from those to which we are accustomed. To take but one striking example: Minoan civilization has two traditional leaders. The greater is Minos, to whom the divine law was revealed on a mountain[55] to fix the pattern of society. The lesser was Daedalus, mastercraftsman of Minos. The obvious analogy of Moses with Minos has been noted long ago,[56] but scholars have failed to see the reflection of Daedalus in Bezalel, mastercraftsman of Moses (Ex. 36.1 — 38.22 ff.). In the artistic Minoan civilization, Daedalus was a necessity. In the unartistic Hebrew tradition, Bezalel might have been omitted.[57] But so strong was the Minoan standard that Hebrew tradition mirrors Daedalus by Bezalel, as well as Minos by Moses. Bezalel's Minoan inspiration is corroborated by the name of a group of his creations: the _kaftôrîm_ (Ex. 37.17, 19, 20, 21, 22), whose connection with Caphtor is clear. The Mosaic structure of Hebrew tradition is not in the manner of Egypt or Mesopotamia, but of the East Mediterranean, whose hub was Crete.

---

[54] Ug. _ṭ_ was pronounced much like Eg. _s_. It is unfortunate that the problems of transliteration impose on the general reader difficulties that have no basis in reality. A more substantial problem is posed by the resemblance of _skty_ and Old Kingdom _msktt_. But we must recognize that cultural interplay between Egypt and the Mediterranean, though accelerated in the second millennium, was already well under way in the third millennium.

[55] Dionysius of Halicarnassus, _Roman Antiquities_ 2:61.

[56] E. g., J. Baikie, _The Sea-Kings of Crete_, London, 3rd. ed., 1920, p. 136.

[57] So dependent were the Hebrews in the material arts that they had to call in the Phoenicians to construct the Temple in Jerusalem.

CHAPTER II

SOCIETY

41. East Mediterranean society had a large class of nobles constituting a check on the power of the king. The epic, which shows little interest in the common man,[58] is addressed to, and sides with, the ruling class. When Thersites (Il. 2:225–42) upbraids King Agamemnon, the poet's sympathy is solidly with the King even though Thersites' tirade is not altogether unjustified. Odysseus accordingly takes Thersites to task and puts him in his place brutally. The same theme occurs in Israel's heroic age; David, in his hour of need, is reviled by Shimei, whom Joab (like Odysseus) would have handled roughly (II Sam. 16.5–9).

42. The divinity of kings (Od. 4:621, 689–92) was a concept that enhanced royal authority. Kret, son of El, was not only divine but even the son of the head of the pantheon,[59] exactly like Sarpedon son of Zeus (Il. 16:522). In Egypt, every Pharaoh was the god Horus incarnate, suckled at the breasts of Isis.[60] Also in Ugarit, the prince, destined to become king, is represented as suckled at the breasts of Asherah and Anath, the divine wet nurses.[61] Royal sucklings, in the act of drinking milk from the nipples of a goddess, are depicted in an ivory panel of a royal bed found at Ugarit.[62] Unlike the Egyptian representative of this theme (with only one suckling), the Ugaritic variant shows two royal sucklings in keeping with textual references to "the two who suck the breast."[63] (Are we to compare the institution of dual kingship such as flourished at Sparta?) "The breast of kings" in Isa. 60.16 shows that the concept of divine kingship was known in Israel too. Against this background, *diotrefês*

---

[58] Contrast the aristocratic atmosphere of the Old Testament with the prominence of common folk in the New Testament.

[59] Text 125:20–21.

[60] Often portrayed in Egyptian art.

[61] Text 128:II:25–28.

[62] The act is carved on an ivory panel of the royal Ugaritic bed published by Cl. Schaeffer, *Illustrated London News*, March 27, 1954, p. 489, fig. 6.

[63] Text 51:III:41, VI:56.

(Il. 2:445; 14:27; 17:685; etc.), frequently applied to kings, does not mean that they were nurtured by Zeus, but rather that they had been qualified for divine kingship by sucking the breasts of a goddess.

43. The deportment and condition of the king were regarded as affecting the whole realm. Od. 19:109–14 states that a good king fears the gods, is lord over many mighty men and upholds justice, with the result that the earth bears grain, the trees are laden with fruit, the flocks multiply, the sea yields fish and the people prosper. The Epic of Kret provides a parallel (though parallels to this theme are well nigh universal); when Kret sins, he becomes ill so that he cannot uphold justice (127:27–54), with the result that drought and famine befall the land (126:III: 12–16).

44. To what extent people were carried away by the fiction of divine kingship is hard to say. All we know is that in epic literature, death, or impending death, raised the problem in Kret's case as to whether El's son could die (125:20–23) and implied in Sarpedon's case that Zeus did not rescue his own son (Il. 16:521–2).

45. One of the features of a heroic age (whose general characteristic is instability combined with decentralization) is lability of leadership. The principle of charismatic (*i. e.*, inspired, nonhereditary) leadership (exemplified in the Book of Judges) is so strong that it enfeebles the incipient institution of kingship. Out of the period of the Judges, Hebrew kingship gradually evolved. Along the way we find the abortive kingship of Abimelech. Saul was more successful but even he did not succeed in implanting the concept of hereditary kingship. His own son Jonathan is represented as accepting the fact that David would become king of Israel. Similarly Telemachus (Od. 1:394–8, 400–4) admits that there are other kings of the Achaeans in Ithaca who may succeed Odysseus, but that in any case he, Telemachus, ought to inherit Odysseus' house and slaves. Though David took the kingship from the house of Saul, David nevertheless felt that Saul's estate should be held by Saul's heirs. Thus rivalry between royal houses was so normal that society had developed a pattern for the proper conduct of the new

29

house toward the old. In the Iliad (13:461; 20:179–86, 306) we see the rivalry between the houses of Priam and of Anchises for the kingship of Troy. Aeneas, son of Anchises, thus aspires to become king of Troy (Il. 20:178–83), and his claim is legitimized by a genealogy representing him as a member of another branch of Priam's family. Just as David's replacement of Saul was justified in theological terms as God's casting off Saul in favor of David, so too the Iliad (20:306–8) explains Aeneas' kingship for generations to come on the ground that Zeus had cast off as odious the race of Priam. This is essentially the doctrine of the divine selection of kings, and comes quite close to the Biblical idea of the Covenant, especially insofar as God promised Abraham and Jacob that kings for the generations to come would issue forth from their loins.[64]

46. It was within the pale of good manners to ask people their genealogy, according to East Mediterranean epic standards. In fact to do so was simply a routine question (e. g., Od. 20:191–3). Eliezer asks Rebecca: "Whose daughter are you?" And she gives a straightforward answer to what was regarded as a natural question: "I am the daughter of Bethuel, son of Milcah, whom the latter bore to Nahor" (Gen. 24.23–24). The Greek parody of Homer, entitled "The Battle of the Frogs and Mice," is of interest in this connection, because it singles out (among other features of Homer that seemed grotesque to the later Greeks) the requesting and reciting of genealogy.[65] The epic emphasis on genealogy has a *raison d'être*; the epic concerns, and was addressed to, the aristocracy, to whom parentage is all important. When Saul participated in ecstatic behavior with a band of prophets, people could not understand how "the Son of Kish" could behave that way (I Sam. 10.11). Note that he is referred to patronymically. And, in the next verse, the question is asked: "Who is their father?" The question is rhetorical, for ecstatic prophets were not well-born. When an aristocrat like Saul, son of Kish, consorts with low-born people, the Hebrew saying was "Is Saul also among the prophets?" (vv. 11–12).

[64] Gen. 17.6, 35.11.

[65] In line 13 a frog inquires of a mouse: "Who are you, stranger? Whence come you to this shore? And who is the one that begot you?"

47. The nature of East Mediterranean epic is such that narrative goes hand in hand with genealogy. The two are so artistically and inextricably combined in Homer[66] that it would be fantastic to rip them asunder into different literary strata. But because in the Pentateuch the same two indispensable and inseparable epic elements of narrative and genealogy are not so closely intertwined, it is customary to attribute the genealogies to a different source (often to P, centuries later) from that of the accompanying narrative (often attributed to the earlier J and E). This separation of genealogy from narrative, however natural it may seem to the modern occidental reader, is untenable once we place the Epic of Israel in its East Mediterranean epic setting.

48. It stands to reason that in a society where noble birth is of great value, low birth and illegitimacy convey a high degree of notoriety, — whence narrative interest. Medon is singled out as the bastard son of godlike Oileus (Il. 13:694); and Medecaste, as a bastard daughter of Priam (Il. 13:171–3). The fact that Perez (ancestor of David!)[67] was born from a union that in any society would raise the eyebrows of ladies and gentlemen (Gen. 38), must be understood against the background of human interest so prized in the epic. Jephthah's being the son of a harlot (Judg. 11.1), far from condemning him, enhances the interest of his rise to leadership.

49. Similarly, precisely because age was respected for its wisdom, it was worthy of note when the young (albeit with appropriate apologies) counseled the old. Diomedes, speaking to his elders (Il. 14:110–2), apologizes to them saying: "Be in no wise vexed and wroth — because in years I am the youngest among you." The same type of rhetorical introduction (though with sarcastic overtones) begins Elihu's speech in Job 32.6 ff.: "I am young of days, and you are aged, therefore I was shy and feared to tell you my view. I said days should speak and multitude of years should teach wisdom. But . . . ." (The dramatic elements in Job, Song of Songs, and Ugaritic text 52, should

---

[66] *E. g.*, the meeting of Glaucus and Diomedes on the battle-field, with the purple passage of Glaucus's genealogy (Il. 6:119–236).

[67] Ruth 4.18–22.

be analyzed together with Greek drama, with reference to their relations with East Mediterranean epic).

50. The day's work began at dawn. In Gen. 32.25–32, there is the tale of Jacob's wrestling with the angel (actually "a deity"; N. B., v. 31), who insists on being released by Jacob at dawn (v. 27). The reason for this insistence (as J. K. Gordon called to my attention) is supplied by a frequent Homeric cliché (Il. 9:706–9; Od. 9:152 ff.; 12:142 ff.; etc.) showing that at dawn people must begin going about their work. In other words, the angel was free to wrestle only "on his own time"; but at dawn he had to commence his official duties.

51 Certain material features of daily life are common to both the Semitic and Greek branches of the epic. Odysseus' cloak of doubled fold (note *diplên* in Od. 19:226, cf. 241, 255) is reminiscent of the Ugaritic Daniel's cloak of double fold (*mizrtm*).[68] Also Telemachus' purple cloak (Od. 4:154) has Semitic parallels; e. g., Ugaritic (*tn*)[69] and Hebrew (*šānî* as in II Sam. 1.24) purple clothes for elegant wear. The source of the dye was Phoenician murex (from which the later Roman royal purple was made).

52. Old Near East legal literature deals with the institution permitting a man to raise his concubine's children of servile rank to the status of full freedom on a par with the children of his wives. Indeed the emergence of leaders from such lowliness is a theme that made for good story telling (§48). Abimelech, the lowest born of his father's offspring, rose to kingship.[70] Saul was of the small tribe of Benjamin, and yet God elevated him to the throne. That this theme (which could occur in real life) was worthy of saga is also reflected in the Odysseus's (Od. 14:199–203) concocting a yarn to the effect that he, though born of a concubine to a man with many sons of a full-fledged wife, had been elevated to full sonship.

53. A trusted servant could be adopted to sonship (alongside a real son) and win from his adoptive father a house and wife

---

[68] *Ugaritic Manual* §§8.41; 20.82.

[69] Text 145:16.

[70] Judg. 8.31; 9.6. Moreover, Gideon claims to be from the poorest clan in Manasseh and the youngest in his family (Judg. 6.15).

(Od. 21:213–6). It happened now and then in real life that a "wise slave would rule over a shameful son, and in the midst of brothers share the estate" (Prov. 17.2). Od. 14:61–66 makes it clear that a good master might give house, land and a good wife to a slave who had worked much for him and whose labor god had prospered. Eliezer, slave of Abraham, is manager of Abraham's household, and Nuzu parallels make it clear that he had been adopted by Abraham.[71] Homeric woman had such a high status (§§72–79) that even a handmaid could be manager of the household until the noble bachelor son would find a noble bride (Od. 15:24–26).

54. Not uncommonly a man might go to his mother's family, where he would find a fosterhome and marry one of the girls there (Il. 11.221–8). This is exactly what is told of Jacob, who found a foster home with Laban (his mother's brother) and eventually married Laban's daughters.[72]

55. The Nuzu tablets and the Patriarchal narratives in Genesis show that the son-in-law might be adopted into the bride's family.[73] This usage may be reflected also in Il. 9:141 ff., where Agamemnon agrees to make Achilles his son-in-law, honored along with Orestes.

56. It was not considered wise to let an only son, on whom the continuity of the line depended, risk the hazards of travel. Eurycleia advises Telemachus not to run the risks of travel since he is an only and beloved son (Od. 2:363–70). This provides an explanation of why Isaac, the only son of Sarah, is not allowed to travel to Paddan-Aram, but instead Eliezer is dispatched (Gen. 24).

57. East Mediterranean epic abounds (§58) in illustrations of what we might call the motif of the Curse of Cain, or of the man whose deeds force him to be a homeless wanderer over the face of the earth. The interesting thing is that he is the object of sympathy no matter how heinous his offense may be. Cain ad-

[71] See my "Biblical Customs and the Nuzu Tablets," *Biblical Archaeologist* 3, 1940, pp. 1–12; the most recent discussion is *Introduction to Old Testament Times*, pp. 100 ff.

[72] Gen. 29.16–28.

[73] See footnote 71 above.

mits his unforgivable guilt and yet God protects him from any that would slay him during his wanderings (Gen. 4:13–15). Thus banishment was considered a sufficient punishment for any crime, even fratricide.

58. Zeus gives some men a mixture of good and evil; but to others he apportions only misfortune so that they wander, mad or hungry, over the face of the earth unhonored by gods or men (Il. 24:529–33). Epeigeus, for example, slew a good man of his own kin, and so, like Cain, became a vagabond (Il. 16:570–4). Also Theoclymenus, by slaying a kinsman, became a wanderer in fear of the avenger's pursuit (Od. 15:272–8). Poseidon punished Odysseus not by killing him but by making him wander away from his native land (Od. 1:74-75). This is a repeated theme in Homer (cf. also Od. 14:379–81, etc.) wherein, often enough, the wanderer finds a foster home. Similarly, Moses killed an Egyptian and, fearing retribution, fled to Midian (Ex. 2.12 ff.), where he found hospitality in Jethro's house and was taken into the family by marrying Jethro's daughter, Zipporah. For a variant of this motif, note that Jacob, fleeing from Esau's wrath, takes refuge in Laban's house and cements relations by marrying Laban's daughters (§62).

59. The foregoing incidents (§§57–58) impinge on a basic facet of Near East society: hospitality. There was no written law, or fixed legislation, in such matters. The plural nouns in Od. 9:215 ("who knew not justices and laws") show that society was in practice regulated not by any rigid written code, but rather by the accumulation of traditions: a sort of common law. All good men offered hospitality whenever the occasion arose; note Od. 3 for Nestor's hospitality, and Od. 4 for Menelaus'. Odysseus anxiously wants to know whether the Phaeacians "love strangers and fear the gods" (Od. 6:121). Cf. also Od. 14:389 where kindness to the stranger stems from the fear of Zeus; and Od. 9:174–6 where people are either (1) cruel, wild and unjust or (2) they love strangers and fear the gods. Similarly, Abraham was apprehensive lest there were no "fear of (the) gods" in Gerar, with the result that the inhabitants of the place might slay him, a stranger (Gen. 20.11). Hospitality is thus the mark of godfearing men.

34

60. The earthly virtue of hospitality is carried over into the divine sphere. Just as Calypso welcomes Hermes, asking what his mission might be, and serving him food and drink, whereupon he delivers his message (Od. 5:87–115), so too does El ask Asherah why she came, whereupon he offers her food and drink, and finally she delivers her message (51:IV:31 ff.). The formalities of entertainment are part of the epic repertoire.

61. A good host would urge the guest to remain (Od. 11:339–40, 350–2), though the guest would refuse because of a task to be accomplished. Menelaus urges Telemachus to prolong his visit for eleven or twelve days, but Telemachus declines (Od. 4:587–99). Judg. 19.4–10 narrates how the Judean father-in-law kept urging his Levite son-in-law to remain day after day as his guest until the latter tore himself away to return home. Gen. 24.56 tells how Eliezer resisted his hosts' urgings and departed, homeward bound.

62. A romantic touch is often injected into the motif of hospitality. Od. 6:110 ff. relates how Odysseus is greeted by maidens in a strange land; and the chief maiden brings him to her father's house with marriage in mind. Moses similarly encounters Jethro's daughters in Midian, and eventually marries one of them (Ex. 2.15–21). Cf. also Jacob's meeting Rachel, eventually to marry her; and Eliezer's meeting Rebecca, though he secured her in marriage not for himself but for Isaac. See §58.

63. East Mediterranean epic often singles out the detail that the male host bids his wife to prepare a meal for the guest. Menelaus bids Helen (and her handmaids) to make ready a meal for Telemachus (Od. 15:92–94); Ugaritic Daniel bids his wife Dantay to do the same for Kothar-and-Hasis (2 Aqht: V:16–25); and Kret bids Hurray prepare a feast for the grandees (128:IV:2–28). It is in this framework that we are to place Abraham's instructions to Sarah upon the arrival of his divine guests: "And Abraham hastened to the tent, unto Sarah and said, 'Rush three seah-measures of fine flour; knead and prepare cakes!' " (Gen. 18.6).

64. Women frequently performed services for the comfort of the guests. When Odysseus is disguised as a stranger, Helen bathes and anoints him (Od. 4:252). Eurycleia washes Odysseus'

35

feet and anoints him with oil (Od. 19:343–507).[74] In Od. 17:88–90, the maids bathe, anoint and dress the guests. In Od. 6:209–10 the girls are ordered to bathe the stranger; actually they give him a cloak and oil, and bid him bathe. He, while accepting their contributions, asks them to stand away so as to spare his shame. Afterwards come the refreshments (:214–50). In general, Homeric hospitality — with its many elements such as pouring water on the stranger's hands, urging him to stay longer, etc. (Od. 3 provides good examples) — is basically the same in the Near East down to the present day, especially among the Bedouin but also among other elements of the population.

65. From the earliest times attested in Near East epic, the parting gift to the stranger homeward bound, is emphasized. Utnapishtim and his wife see to it that Gilgamesh does not go home empty handed, but bearing gifts including the precious elixir of youth (Gilgamesh Epic 11:240–70). The gift was indeed the due of strangers (Od. 9:267–8; cf. 10:17–24), especially if they were homeward bound (Od. 10:66). The host owed recompense to the guest who enriched him with grace of words and a heart of wisdom (Od. 11:367).[75] Menelaus and Helen gave gifts, as well as wished a safe return, to Telemachus (Od. 15:51–53, 75–76, 82–85, 99–132). Even a poor swineherd owes a gift (be it ever so small) to a visiting beggar (Od. 14:57–59). Penelope tells the incognito Odysseus that she would indeed give to him (apparently a stranger and a guest) such a gift that men would call him blessed (Od. 19:309–11). This explains the range of meaning of Hebrew $b^e r\bar{a}k\bar{a}(h)$, literally "blessing" but in certain contexts (e. g., Judg. 1.15) "gift."

66. It is clear from the preceding paragraph (cf. also Od. 8:387) that showering gifts on departing guests was a feature to which East Mediterranean people attached great weight. (This is still true in the Near East, where $bah\check{s}\hat{\imath}\check{s}$[76] is indispensable in

---

[74] Cf. Luke 7.37–46 for the persistence of these customs into later Hellenistic times.

[75] In a world without newspapers (to say nothing of radio and television), the stranger is the chief source of news too.

[76] It is difficult to translate this word because of its range of meaning, from the most innocent and legitimate gift to the most sinister of bribes.

nearly all human relations.) It is an honor to the giver, who shows thereby his generosity, and an honor to the receiver "blessed" (§65) therewith. Od. 11:355–61 shows that the gifts enhance the guest's honor when he returns home. This puts the gifts showered by the Egyptians upon the Hebrews on the eve of the Exodus (3.21–22; 12.35–36) in a new light. The departure of the Hebrews, to be honorable, had to have the bestowal of lavish gifts. Departure without them would have been shameful according to East Mediterranean values. That this feature had long enjoyed favored status in Egyptian literature is illustrated in the Shipwrecked Sailor, in which the fabulous serpent showered gifts upon the Sailor so that his homecoming was honorable. It is interesting to note that Odysseus (Od. 14:285–6) says he got wealthy from gifts given to him in Egypt.

67. Inasmuch as hospitality was the cornerstone of decent society and of godfearing men, breaches in hospitality made for good storytelling on the principle that "man bites dog" is more newsworthy than "dog bites man." Antinous rebukes Eumaeus for bringing in a beggar, thus: "Have we not enough vagabonds — that you bid this fellow too?" (Od. 17:375–9). This situation and turn of the phrase remind one of the Philistine King Achish, who when seeing the stranger David acting insane, says to his courtiers: "Behold, you see a man raving. Why do you bring him to me? Do I lack crazy folk that you must bring this to rave on me? Must this come to my house?" (I Sam. 21.15–16). Vagabonds, even crazy ones, were entitled to hospitality, but in too great numbers they could become a burden. Antinous and Achish might possibly have been less hospitable than they should; but men in their position might also have had a house or palace so full of strangers that they could not take on any more.

68. Wicked men could abuse hospitality as an occasion for perpetrating treachery. Aegisthus invited Agamemnon to a feast and slew him (Od. 11:409–11). Conversely, the guest Ishmael murdered his host Gedaliah at a feast (Jer. 41.1–2). These two illustrations of violating the guest-host relationship are given as reprehensible. But this is not always the case. Jael slew Sisera, whom she had received as a guest, but her deed is given as

37

heroic (Judg. 5.6, 24–27). However much we sympathize with Odysseus against the wooers, there is something less than universal virtue in the way he closed the door on them to prevent their escape, while using deception to get the lethal bow for massacring them (Od. 21:234–41, 381–7). That his deeds were considered criminal even by his own community is plain enough from Od. 24:426–37. And yet the public took unmitigated delight in the story. A re-examination of Jehu's purge shows striking analogies. Jehu invited the Baalists to a sacrificial feast (II Kings 10.19) with intent to slay those who accepted his treacherous invitation. He prevented their escape by posting armed guards with orders to kill (v. 24). Then he had the whole multitude slain in cold blood (v. 25). To the reader of Kings, the story is presented as a heroic accomplishment. That it was nevertheless a crime according to Israelite morality is clear from Hos. 1.4; cf. *Introduction to Old Testament Times*, pp. 209–10.

69. Deception has a reputable place in the *mores* of the epic (in sharp contrast to the ethics of an Amos or Socrates). The great goddess Anath herself had a reputation that evoked from the Ugaritic hero Aqhat the taunt that she was a cheat and liar (2 Aqht:VI:34–35). The goddess Athena and her mortal favorite Odysseus were the more devoted to each other because of their guileful characters. The Patriarchal heroes are so guileful that uninitiated readers, unaware of the epic background and standards, are often shocked by Jacob's deceiving Isaac, Esau and Laban.[77]

70. It is not my intention to dwell on attenuated parallels which call for the exercise of highly refined acumen. The reason for reducing such parallels to a minimum at this time is not that they are not worthwhile, but only that at this stage we do better to stress the numerous clear parallels. First things come first. Yet as an illustration of the distorted (but in my opinion probable) parallel, I call the reader's attention to the following observation of J. K. Gordon: Od. 9:413–65 tells how the wily Odysseus deceived the blind Polyphemus by using a fleece; with which we may compare the wily Rachel's and Jacob's deception

---

[77] See *Introduction to Old Testament Times*, pp. 114 ff.

of the blind Isaac by a fleece (Gen. 27). The distortion is apparent in that, while the fleece of the Odyssey is on a living animal, that of Genesis is worn by Jacob.[78]

71. Fratriarchal elements are well known in Elamite, Hurrian, Hittite, Ugaritic and Hebrew society; see my "Fratriarchy in the Old Testament," *Journal of Biblical Literature* 54, 1935, pp. 223–31. When Circe is first called the "sister of Aeetes" (Od. 10:137), and only thereafter follow the names of their father and mother, we are dealing with fratronymy, such as "sister of Lotan, Timna" (Gen. 36.22) and "sister of Tubal-cain, Naamah" (Gen. 4.22). The test passage for differentiating "fratriarch" (Heb. *rôš*) from "firstborn" (Heb. *b^{e}kôr*) is I Chron. 26.10, which tells us "Shimri was the fratriarch, though not the firstborn, for his father appointed him fratriarch."

72. The prominence of woman in a society full of fratriarchy, inevitably produced phenomena that we may well call "sororarchy." In I Chron. 7.18, *'^{a}hôtô hammôleket*, "his sororarch" (literally, "his ruling sister") shows that the institution was recognized and could be expressed terminologically. When Octavia, daughter of Kret, is elevated in rank over her seven older brothers (128:III:16), she becomes the sororarch of her siblings. It is against the social background reflected in epic literature, that we are to reconsider the sociology of the Book of Job. Job's daughters, as well as sons, are his heirs (Job 42.15). Special prominence is given to his daughters, who are named (Job 42.14), though his sons are not. Cf. §76.

73. The high status of East Mediterranean woman is especially noticeable in Crete, where women are repeatedly depicted as equal partners of men in all sorts of activities, including the dangerous sport of bull-grappling.[79] Od. 11 (note especially

---

[78] The link is supplied by a Moroccan folktale of a hero who escapes from a one-eyed foe, by blinding him and then wearing a fleece to evade him; cf. G. Germain, *Genèse de l'Odyssée*, Paris, 1954, pp. 58 ff. The distribution (Greek. Hebrew, Berber) confirms the Mediterranean character of the theme.

[79] Bullfighting probably reached Spain at an early date as a result of the diffusion of Minoan culture. That the sport took on a new character in Spain is only natural. Each nation transforms its cultural heritage. Bullfighting in southern France, though derived from the same Minoan source, is different

lines: 328-9, 385-6) shows a high proportion of distinguished women's departed spirits interviewed by Odysseus; moreover, they precede the men's spirits.

74. The "wise woman" appears in Homer; e. g., wise Penelope (Od. 14:373) and wise Aegialeia (Il. 5:412). This is not a coinage of the poet, but a widespread concept. The Hebrew "wise woman" was a highly valued member of society, whose services were required in the highest circles. The Wise Woman of Tekoa (II Sam. 14.2 ff.) was sought out for a delicate mission in the royal court. A town could entrust its leadership to a wise woman at the most critical moment in the community's history (II Sam. 20.16 ff.).

75. In the epic, woman is often represented as endowed with religious insight. It was Helen, and not the men present, who interpreted an omen and prophesied (Od. 15:171-8). The natural psychic proclivities of woman go, often enough in real life, with religious expression, and woman's gift of prophecy is familiar. Pughat of Ugarit is intuitive; her extra-sensory perception is reflected in her epithet: "knowing the course of the stars." In the Bible, there are prophetesses including late ones, such as Huldah in the days of Josiah. But it is in the heroic age that prophetesses are prominent in Israel. Miriam, sister of Moses, is a prophetess in her own right (Ex. 15.20). Deborah was prophetess and ruler of her people.

76. The epic premium on daughters (§72) is reflected in the mythology. In Ugarit, Baal has three daughters who are named (Ṭly, Arṣy, Pdry), while his seven (or climactically, eight) sons are not named. (Cf. the daughters of Zeus in Il. 9:508-12).[80]

77. Antinous' motive in seeking the hand of Penelope, is through her to become king of Ithaca (Od. 22:52). The crown was thus transmissible through the widow of a king. Similar social customs are, to be sure, widespread. For other East Mediterranean examples, we may note Absalom's presumption to the

again from the Spanish variety. There is room for investigating the spread of Minoan civilization far afield (even beyond the Pillars of Hercules). See G. W. Elderkin, *Zagreus in Ancient Basque Religion*, Princeton University Store, 1952.

[80] For the epic evidence, see §72 above.

throne by appropriating David's concubines; the temerity in Abner's appropriation of Saul's concubine Rizpah; and in Adonijah's desire to wed David's handmaid Abishag.[81]

78. The deification of important women appears in the epic. Zeus made Ariadne deathless and ageless for Dionysus (Hesiod, Theogony 948–9). Sometimes the heroine is regarded as divine from the start, so that her mortal husband is favored by the gods for her sake. Od. 4:569 states that Menelaus enjoyed divine favor because he was married to Zeus' own daughter, Helen. Goddesses are more beautiful than mortal women.[82] They are also immortal and ageless (Hesiod, Theogony 277, 305; Od. 5:218). Helen, daughter of Zeus, thus surpassed womankind in beauty; nor did age diminish her charms. Twenty years after Helen had deserted Menelaus (Il. 24:765–6), she was still such a paragon of loveliness that men from many isles and coasts were fighting far from home for her sake. To be sure, the number "twenty" is conventional (§182); cf. Jacob's twenty years' sojourn with Laban (Gen. 31.38) and Samson's rule over Israel for twenty years (Judg. 15.20); but "twenty years" always designates a very long period. Odysseus comes home twenty years after he had left Penelope and their baby son (Od. 2:175–6); but she is still so beautiful that her halls are full of wooers. This puts the story of Sarah in a new light. She was ninety years old (Gen. 17.17) and yet kings could not resist her feminine pulchritude; see Gen. 20.2 ff. for king Abimelech taking Sarah into his harem. The apparent contradiction between Sarah's age and sex-appeal can most easily be explained in the light of East Mediterranean epic tradition. In the Ur-Patriarchal narratives, Sarah was probably divine (perhaps "the daughter of El," even as Helen was "the daughter of Zeus") and, while monotheistic scruples have eliminated the outright statement from our *textus receptus*, her agelessness and beauty reflect the fiction of her divinity. This finds further support in Gen. 11.29: "Abram and Nahor took for themselves wives; the name of Abram's wife was Sarai; and the name of Nahor's wife was

---

[81] II Sam. 3.7; I Kings 2.13–25.

[82] Od. 5:215–7 brings out the superior beauty of goddesses

Milcah, daughter of Haran father of Milcah and father of
Iscah." The aristocratic mood of the epic calls for genealogy.
Milcah's paternity is given; Sarai's is conspicuously absent. Also
Deborah, wife of Lappidoth, (Judg. 4.4) has no patronymic. It
looks very much as if it were normal for the outstanding heroines
such as Helen, Sarah and Deborah, to claim divine parentage.
That the divine parentage of heroes occurs in Israelite saga is
proved by the matronymic "Shamgar, son of Anath" (Judg. 5.6).
Shamgar, like Achilles, is the son of a goddess; moreover, the
warlike Anath is more appropriate than the gentler Thetis.

79. Woman in the epic was often equal or superior to man
in battle. The Amazons (Il. 3:189) are not the only examples.
Pughat of Ugarit avenged with the sword the death of her
brother (1 Aqht: 190–224). Hebrew epic (Judg. 5) portrays
Deborah as the leader of the hosts in battle, and Jael as the
slayer of the foemen's general. The theme persists into the saga
of the evil Abimelech, whose skull was fractured by a woman
(Judg. 9.53). Woman in actual life can be (and doubtless often
was in those times) violent physically. The Assyrian law code
leaves no doubt as to the dangerous action of which women
were capable.[83] But in Old Testament history, the portrayal of
women as heroic or violent, on a par with strong and dangerous
men, is limited to the heroic age.

80. Maidens might go strolling in search of a husband.
Nausicaa is portrayed thus in Od. 6:1 ff., amongst her (:84)
maids. It is possible that Gen. 34.1–2 reflects similar usages and
should be translated: "And Dinah, daughter of Leah, whom
the latter bore to Jacob, went out to be seen[84] among the
daughters of the land, and Shechem saw her . . . ." Shechem
became enamored of Dinah and sought her hand in marriage.

81. Often in the epic, a well born bride is to be won, not
by gifts and great bridal price, but by deeds of valor (Od.
14:211–2). Neleus refuses to give his daughter Pero to any
except the man who accomplishes a specified act of bravery
(Od. 11:287–90). Othryoneus would wed the princess Cassandra,

[83] Tablet A, section 8; paralleled in Deut. 25.11–12.

[84] The infinitive of the simple conjugation is neutral; and may be translated passively (instead of actively as is usually done).

daughter of Priam, without gifts but through mighty deeds of war (Il. 13:366). David won Michal not by paying a conventional bride price, but by slaying a hundred (var., two hundred) Philistines and bringing back their foreskins as the evidence (I Sam. 18.25–27; II Sam. 3.14). Also Othniel won Achsah, the daughter of Caleb, as his bride by capturing Kiriath-Sepher (Judg. 1.12–13).

82. Hand in hand with the bride price went the dowry, given by the bride's father to the groom. Kingly fathers were often in a position to present kingly dowries, such as one or more cities. Pharaoh gave his daughter who had married King Solomon, the city of Gezer as a dowry (I Kings 9.16). Agamemnon offered seven cities as his daughter's dowry (Il. 9:149–52).[85]

83. Widows could, upon remarriage, deprive their existing children of their patrimony (Od. 15:21–23). This was common enough in the Semitic world to judge from the last wills and testaments of husbands who let their wives inherit on condition that the property would not go to a strange man. This is attested, for example, in the tablets from Ugarit and Nuzu.[86] The widow would be given power to show preference, in willing the property, toward any of her sons by her dead husband, but she could not pass on the estate to an outsider. This secured filial respect for her without risking the alienation of the property outside the deceased's family.

84. The question of marital irregularities must be considered in the light of the evolution of the epic. Long before the Homeric poems or Biblical books were composed in their present form, as large compositions, the bards of the East Mediterranean were going from banquet to banquet, entertaining lords and ladies with songs (Od. 13:8–9, 25–28). Such audiences, on such occasions, demanded amusement so that the songs had to be full of action and spice. Much of the action has to do with battle

---

[85] The motif of cities given as a dowry continues to reverberate into late oriental literature; e. g., the *Laughable Stories* of Bar Hebraeus (N. B. the tale of the owl that would give a dowry of ruined towns).

[86] I have discussed these texts in *Ugaritic Literature*, Rome, 1949, pp 126–7 and in *Zeitschrift für Assyriologie* 43, 1936, pp. 162–3. The principle is enunciated in Hammurabi's Code §150.

(§§94–122). Much of the spice has to do with sexual irregularities (§§86–92).

85. Even so innocent a topic as personal beauty is limited to the epic age in the historic books of the Old Testament, from Genesis through Kings. Prior to Solomon, men and women are often singled out as handsome; e. g., Sarah (Gen. 12.11), Rachel (Gen. 29.17), Joseph (Gen. 39.6), David (I Sam. 16.12), Abigail (I Sam. 25.3), Bath-sheba (II Sam. 11.2), Absalom (II Sam. 14.25), two Tamars (II Sam. 13.1 and 14.27), etc. Solomon's reign marks the growth of annalistic sources and the drastic reduction of epic sources, in Hebrew historiography. David's reign shows a combination of both types of sources. Prior to David, the sources may well have been limited to oral tradition, mainly epical.

86. Spicy *Frauengeschichten*, like the topic of personal beauty, and for the same reason (§85), are common in the historic books from Genesis through Kings, down through David's reign (§§87–92), whereupon they come to an abrupt stop.

87. Scandal is the spice of epic; and it is spiciest when it concerns the great. The noble East Mediterranean audience was not interested in the scandals of riff-raff, but only of the aristocracy. It is against this background that Reuben's seduction of his father's concubine is to be understood. The firstborn of Jacob was no mean figure and his sin was not without social interest. It was used etiologically to explain his tribe's misfortunes, for the offense got him his father's curse instead of blessing.[87] It has not escaped the attention of scholars that Phoenix (Il. 9:444–57) is a counterpart of Reuben in this respect. He too got a paternal curse instead of blessing for seducing his father's concubine. His motivation is interesting because the same or a similar one may have been expunged from the epic precursor of the Biblical account: Phoenix committed his sin not out of lust but in order to alienate the affections of the concubine from his father, who was neglecting Phoenix's mother because of infatuation with the concubine. Note that in Gen. 30.14–17, where Jacob's wives vie for his marital attentions, it is Reuben who is involved in securing preferential treatment for this mother.

---

[87] Gen. 35.22; 49.4.

88. The motif of recovering the stolen belle makes its first recorded appearance in East Mediterranean epic. While it is absent from the earlier literatures of Egypt and Mesopotamia, it is so popular in the East Mediterranean that we may consider it a virtually indispensable part of every kingly cycle (§20). In the Iliad, the abduction of Helen is the cause of the Trojan War. The end of the War brought Helen back to the arms of her rightful husband, King Menelaus. In Ugaritic, King Kret must wage war to win back his rightful wife, the Princess Hurray. King David, too, must get back his rightful wife, the Princess Michal.[88]

89. The public could not get enough of this theme. Sarah was twice wrested from her husband, Abraham, by kings: by the Pharaoh and by Abimelech of Gerar. The same Philistine Abimelech or his subjects came close to taking Rebecca away from Isaac.[89] We should not assume, as is usually done, that these "repetitions" are due to bad editing. The public wanted to hear this motif again and again about the same as well as about different heroines; in the same as well as in different compositions. In the Iliad, not only is Helen taken from Menelaus, but also Briseis from Achilles. In the case of Briseis, she is restored untouched to her man (Il. 19:263), as is Sarah to Abraham (Gen. 20.3–4).

90. In a heroic age, characterized by incessant (though often petty) warfare, women must often have been carried off by raiding parties. I Sam. 30 describes how the Amalekites burned David's town of Ziklag, during David's absence, and made off with everything including the women (v. 2). David overtook the marauders and retrieved his two wives (v. 18). We have no outside sources for checking the historicity of this particular incident. But we may safely assume that such incidents were common enough in those days.

91. In the earlier literatures of Egypt and Mesopotamia, the heroes show no romantic interest in their women. Sexual exploits and formal marriage occur, but nothing remotely akin to passionate devotion or attachment is recorded. Romantic marriage

[88] II Sam. 3.14.
[89] Gen. 12.15; 20.2; 26.8–10.

45

is, however, typical of East Mediterranean epic. In addition to the examples in §§88–90, we may note how Rebecca was fetched from afar for Isaac, and how Jacob went through numerous trials and chagrins to win the girl of his heart, Rachel. David's affair with Bathsheba is the most circumstantial account we have of a romance fraught with sinful lust. We need not go into the question of how factual the story is. That kings now and then appropriated the beautiful wives of their subjects is all too factual. That some of the kings of divided Israel and Judah engaged in romantic love (permitted and forbidden) is a foregone conclusion. But post-Solomonic historiography shows absolutely no interest in such matters. Romantic marriage in Israel is recorded only during the heroic age.

92. The wrath of Achilles (Il. 1:1) was caused by Agamemnon's seizing Achilles' beloved Briseis. This wrath is of basic importance in the drama of the Iliad. On account of it many brave Achaeans lost their lives. Homer may have developed this theme into the noblest story in all epic literature, but he did not invent the theme. It occurs also in a story of Samson, who, because his Philistine wife had been taken from him and given to another man, flew into a rage and wreaked havoc on the Philistines by burning their crops and orchards. Nor did his wrath subside until it had taken a heavy toll of Philistine lives (Judg. 15.1–8). We cannot help noticing that the wrath of Achilles and the wrath of Samson unfold in Caphtorian milieus; the one in the Mycenean, the other in the Philistine, segment of Caphtorian culture.

CHAPTER III

WAR

93. It was believed that gods as well as men fought in war. Thus the battles of ancient Israel could be narrated in a composition entitled "The Book of the Wars of Yahwe" (Num. 21.14), for Yahwe participated in the battles of his people, just as the Greek pantheon took sides and participated in the Trojan War. Accordingly the prayer for peace could not be limited to "goodwill among men"; instead Il. 18:107 reads "so may strife perish among gods and men." The Ugaritic Cycle of Baal and Anath is full of battle and brawls.

94. The bellicose Anath lays low her victims by hurling furniture at them ('nt:II:20–22, 36–37) including chairs, tables and footstools. The throwing of footstools in brawls is a recurrent feature in the Odyssey (17:230–2, 409–19, 462; 18:394).

95. Military commanders were grouped in threes (Od. 14:470–1). Il. 12:85–107 is particularly instructive in this regard for there we are told of five triads of officers leading the troops of Troy and her allies. One triad consists of Hector and Polydamus, with whom Kebriones serves as the "third" (:91, cf. 95). This use of "third" clarifies the Hebrew word *šālîš*, "officer," derived from the numeral *šālôš*, "3." Each East Mediterranean military contingent had three officers. In the case of the fifth triad, Sarpedon is called superior to his two associates (:101–4), just as Abishai the brother of Joab is famed as superior to his two colleagues in II Sam. 23.18–19 and I Chron. 11.20–21. (For the triads of David's heroic commanders see II Sam. 23 and I Chron. 11.)

96. As distinct from Mesopotamian annals, in which no man but the king gets any credit, East Mediterranean tradition glories in giving credit to the officers who contribute to the victory. In the Iliad glory is by no means restricted to King Agamemnon nor to any other individual; not even the peerless warrior Achilles. The repertoire of East Mediterranean epic includes "catalogues of the heroes" recounting their names and deeds (e. g., Il. 4:457 ff.; II Sam. 23; I Chron. 11).

97. This decentralization of the honors is appropriate to the ancient mode of battle, which was not so much a unified operation but rather an action fragmentized into numerous little combats between small teams or even between individuals. This type of warfare is depicted on battle scenes in Mesopotamian and Egyptian art. To be sure, even in early times, the troops might march out to battle in highly organized formation. The phalanx appears fully developed on the old Sumerian Stela of the Vultures; yet on ancient monuments we also see the combat fragmentized into separate frays between individuals. The apparent contradiction is to be explained chronologically; the battle began in organized and unified array, but as the struggle developed, it split up into little fighting units. The early Egyptian order of battle seems to be decentralized, to judge from the slate palette of King Narmer, who ruled around 3000 B. C., when Upper and Lower Egypt were welded into united nationhood. The palette portrays the banners of the different contingents. This emphasis on decentralization may explain why the Egyptians nurtured a tradition which accorded glory in writing, not only to the Pharaoh but also to his officers who led the contingents. Thus some of the generals who fought under Thothmes III have left texts celebrating their bravery and triumphs. The habit of proclaiming the glory of officers appears in Egypt before the Hebrews and Greeks come on the historic scene. It is therefore not unlikely that Egypt contributed to the East Mediterranean the custom of celebrating the feats of heroes as well as of the king.

98. The East Mediterranean had an elite type of warrior for whom no place is made in modern warfare; to wit, ambidextrous troops. Such was Asteropaeus who "hurled with both spears at once, for he was one who could use both hands alike" (Il. 21: 162–3). This shows that the "right and left handed" archers and slingers of I Chron. 12.2 are respectively not two sets of soldiers, but one.[90]

99. Long hair was associated with heroic strength. How widespread this notion was is hard to say. The Gilgamesh Epic states that the mighty Enkidu had long hair like a woman; and the glyptic art represents his hair in keeping with the texts. The hair of Gilgamesh, though not as long as Enkidu's, is at least long enough to be curled on both sides. Il. 20:39 associates the fighting strength of the god Phoebus with his unshorn locks. The warrior Euphorbus has hair like the Graces, with tresses braided with silver and gold (Il. 17:51–52). The Achaean warriors are often called the "longhaired" (Il. 2:323, 443; cf. also 4:261; etc.). This style is to be compared with the Keftiu (=Caphtorians/Cretans) as depicted in the tombs of Senmut

[90] *I. e.*, One category of ambidextrous archers, and one category of ambidextrous slingers.

and Rekhmare. Their hair, in Senmut's tomb, is arranged in long tails down their shoulders. In Rekhmare's tomb, their long hair hangs down to their waist, and some is twisted into knots and curled on top. It is interesting to note that precisely during the epic age of Israel, long hair is a feature of the heroic male. An issue is made of such hair in Ex. 32.25. It also figures in the Song of Deborah (Judg. 5.2). The most famous example, however, is Samson, whose great strength depended on his long curls, seven in number (Judg. 16.19). (Samson's case suggests that the cultic institution of the Nazirite has East Mediterranean ramifications at least as concerns the prohibition against shaving the head.) Finally, Absalom's long hair figures prominently in his epic story, just before the close of the heroic age of Israel. The topic does not recur in the subsequent history of Israel and Judah.

100. The most prized arm of the fighting forces was the horse-drawn chariotry. The greatest heroes, such as Achilles and Hector, were chariot warriors. Each chariot was drawn by two horses, but an extra horse was part of the fully equipped chariot. Thus Achilles' two steeds were Xanthus and Balius, with Pedasus as the third (or as the Greek puts it *en de parêoriê-sin*; Il. 16:152). The Kret Epic also specifies the chariot equipped with three steeds (Krt:140, 285-6).

101. Morale in war was bolstered by claiming high purposes. The Cypria (no. 3) states that the aim of the Trojan War was to relieve the earth of oppression. History probably inherits some of its moralizing on war from a more heroic past. The battle of Gilgamesh and Enkidu against the draconic Humbaba is justified by the claim that it is for the purpose of wiping out evil from the land.

102. A psychological device for fanning the flame of morale was to proclaim a fast for victory (Il. 19:198–213; I Sam. 14.24).[91]

103. The Iliad repeatedly illustrates how the commanders had to build morale in the ranks by chiding, begging, coercing and exhorting. Demoralized troops would not even refrain from

[91] As a field archeologist in the Near East, I found that normally peaceful Muslim laborers often become pugnacious during the arduous daytime fasts during Ramadan.

weeping. Il. 2:289–90 states that the Achaean troops wailed like children or widows for home. And Od. 10:410–5 narrates that when Odysseus returned to his ship, his comrades thronged about him weeping like calves that with constant lowing run about their mothers. Cf. Ugaritic 128:I:5–7 where we read of soldiers moaning for their mothers as a cow lows for her calf.

104. Feigning madness to evade military duty is as old as history, and is still with us. But, whereas it is now hardly applicable to heroes, it was so on occasion in East Mediterranean epic. According to the Cypria, Odysseus pretended to be insane to evade participation in the Trojan War. David's feigned madness in the presence of King Achish of Gath is possibly in the same tradition (I Sam. 21.11–16), at least if there was originally some connection with I Sam. 29 telling of David's exemption from serving with Achish in battle.[92]

105. Scouting and spying were considered worthy of saga. Il. 10:204 ff. tells of sending out a spy. Od. 9:83–104 and 10:102 narrate how a pair of men would be sent to spy out the land, accompanied by a third man serving as a herald. Joshua sent spies ahead into Canaan; they came back with wondrous reports such as of giants in the land. The motif of spies coming back with an amazing tale was welcome in the epic repertoire; cf. also Od. 9:83–104 where Odysseus' spies report on the land of the lotus eaters.

106. The diplomatic machinery existed for averting war through negotiation. Not only do we find heralds to deliver messages, to make proposals for peace and to exploit speech before resorting to violence, in the Greece of Thucydides, but already in the world of Homer. Still earlier, the Epic of Kret abounds in evidence of heralds who in pairs offered peace terms and gifts so that the invader might be induced to return home and call off the war. Hector thinks of sharing the contents of Troy with the Achaeans so as to liquidate the war (Il. 22:117–8) through diplomacy instead of further fighting. Similarly, King Pbl, through his emissaries, offers Kret a number of lavish gifts including a "share of the place" if Kret will depart in peace.

---

[92] In any case the parallel stands insofar as David's simulated insanity was to avoid danger.

107. Strife and feuds could be eliminated if the wronged party accepted blood money (Il. 9:632–6) or ransom. Refusal of ransom meant a fight to the death, and was therefore a favorite theme of the bards who had to make the story as exciting as possible. Od. 22:61–67 has Odysseus refusing any ransom and insisting on the death of the wooers. Judges 5.19 conveys the terror of a fight to a finish by stating that the kings of Canaan would accept no bribe of silver to call off the war. The Kret Epic (like the Iliad) has the hero refusing any settlement of gold, silver or precious possessions.

108. A blood bath could be circumvented by settling the issue through a fight between champions of each side; cf. Il. 3:59 ff. and 7:74–91. The challenge of a champion to single combat was accompanied by an exchange of oratory (Il. 7:225–43; etc.). The challenge of Goliath to fight a champion of Israel was met by David after a characteristic word-battle. The epic nature of the fight between David and Goliath is evident not only from its dramatic form but also from the Biblical evidence that the story was transferred to David from one of his officers.[93] Sometimes the champions were more than one in number for each side; thus in the strife between the armies of Joab and Abner, twenty-four champions fought, twelve to a side.[94]

109. Even when wars were fought out by entire armies, the fighting is often represented in terms of individual combat with words exchanged between the contestants (Il. 5:274–89; etc.). The discourse between Patroclus and Hector, or between Achilles and Hector, are but two of many examples in the Iliad. The dialogue between Asahel and Abner in the heat of battle (II Sam. 2.20–22) is a Hebrew example.

110. A feature to enhance the interest of combat is the disguise of the hero, who, notwithstanding, meets his death in battle. Patroclus goes into the fray disguised in the armor of Achilles (Il. 16:40 ff.) but meets his death. While this feature does not occur in the heroic age of Israel, it is highlighted in the account of Ahab who, though disguised, meets his doom

[93] See *Introduction to Old Testament Times*, pp. 146–7.
[94] II Sam. 2.14–16.

51

(in fulfilment of a prophecy[95]) during the battle with the Arameans at Ramoth-gilead. At this juncture we may observe that the epic tradition continues to enrich Hebrew historiography in a number of episodes preserved in the account of the kings of Judah and Israel. This is the case especially when the narratives in Kings are the most interesting. Naboth's vineyard, the wars of Ahab, the purge of Jehu, the doom of Athaliah, the speech of Rabshakeh; in short, the most memorable and stirring passages of I and II Kings represent historiography in the epic manner. The notable speeches in Herodotus and Thucydides hark back to the epic speeches such as abound in the Iliad; the same holds for the speech of Rabshakeh.

111. Some of the Homeric clichés (including those describing combat), re-echo an older Oriental parallelistic formula. For instance, "he struck him on the head, above (*hyper*) the ear" (Il. 15:433) reflects an original that is represented also in Ugaritic. Thus "he struck him twice on the head, yea thrice above (*'l*) the ear" (3 Aqht:33–34; cf. :22–23). The Greek incidentally clarifies an obscurity in the Ugaritic; *'l* can mean "upon" as well as "above, over" but Greek *hyper* fixes its meaning in this formula as "above, over."

112. Il. 24:663–4 (cf. :778–87) shows that the epic repertoire included the fact that during a siege it became impossible for the defenders to fetch wood from the surrounding country. This necessitated the arranging of a truce between the Achaeans and Trojans for gathering wood and celebrating Hector's funerary rites. That the stoppage of wood gathering during a siege is not introduced into the Iliad as a Greek innovation is indicated by Krt:110–2, 212–5 where the same stoppage is singled out.

113. The epic places the ties of friendship above the conduct of war. Il. 6:212–36 shows that men who had antecedents uniting them in bonds of friendship, could, even though they were on opposite sides in the war, confirm by a pact their friendship and swear not to injure each other in the fray. (For the foe is always numerous enough for two friends on opposite sides to

[95] Prophets were common figures in military and political circles throughout Near East antiquity. They are attested in Homer, Bible, Mari tablets, Lachish ostraca, etc.

avoid one another.) Moreover, the pact is solemnized by exchanging armor. Similarly, the friendship of David and Jonathan transcends the war between their houses. A striking parallel to Homer is Jonathan's gift of his armor to David (I Sam. 18.4).

114. Achilles compares his comrade Patroclus with a girl (Il. 16:7 ff.), reminding us of Gilgamesh's love for Enkidu as for a woman (Gilg. Epic 2:31 ff.; 1:v:47, vi:1 ff.). That this (to us unmanly) attitude was firmly entrenched in Near East epic is shown by its presence in the Book of Jashar (excerpted in II Sam. 1.17 ff.) where David proclaims that Jonathan's love was sweeter to him than the love of women (v. 26).

115. When a hero was wounded, he might, like Glaucus, hide behind a wall, so that none of the enemy might see him smitten and boast over him (Il. 12:390–1). The last phrase is reminiscent of Saul's reason for committing suicide; death was better than letting the foe abuse him (I Sam. 31.4).

116. Side by side with a noble sentiment of charity and sportsmanship toward the foe (§§22–23, 175), the epic makes room for sarcastic gloating over his ruin. With Idomeneus' sarcasm toward his fallen enemy Othryoneus (Il. 13:374–82), compare the Hebrew bard's mockery of Sisera's mother who waits in vain for her dead son's return (Judg. 5.28–31).

117. The epic repertoire includes the fact that at nightfall the commanders could call off an unfinished battle (Il. 7:279–302; II Sam. 2.24–28).

118. For pathos, the poet had at his disposal the theme of retrieving the corpses of slain heroes for funerary rites (Il. 11:257; etc.). The recovery of Patroclus by the Achaeans, and of Hector by the Trojans, for appropriate funerals, are famous illustrations in the Iliad. Od. 5:307–10 preserves the tradition that Odysseus fought to recover the corpse of Achilles. Hebrew epic tells, in variant traditions, of the recovery of Saul and Jonathan for condign rites. I Chron. 10.9–11 relates how Saul's body and armor were taken to Philistia for display, and his head was impaled at Beth-Dagon, whence the men of Jabesh-gilead retrieved the bodies of Saul and his sons. The version in I Sam. 31:8–13 relates that the corpses of Saul and his sons were burned before their bones were buried. This burning is often emended away by the critics, but that it is correct should have been realized precisely because it is out of keeping with normative Semitic burial customs.[96] It is typical of East Mediterranean usage in the heroic age (e. g., the burning of Patroclus or of Hector). Saul's death in battle during the Philistine period, took place at the right time and in the right locale and milieu for these striking Homeric parallels.

119. For the decapitation and the impaling of either the head or body of the vanquished on a city wall, see Il. 18:176–7 and I Sam. 31.9–10.

120. Also attested in both Greek and Hebrew epic is the mourning for slain heroes by the leading surviving hero (thus for Patroclus by Achilles in Il. 18:23–27 and for Saul and Jonathan by David in II Sam. 1.17 ff.) and by the women (Il. 19:287–300; II Sam. 1.24).

121. Innocent women and children were all too often the victims of brutality in time of war. The fear that an Achaean would dash Hector's little son from a wall (Il. 24:734–5) fits in with Hebrew references to the dashing of babies by the foe (II Kings 8.12; Isa. 13.16, 18; Hos. 10.14; Nah. 3.10). The killing of unborn children in Il. 6:55–60 is matched by the ripping open of pregnant women in II Kings 15.16; Hos. 14.1; Amos 1.13.

122. Nor were the prisoners of war always exempt from barbarous treatment. Achilles doomed twelve Trojan nobles to having their throats cut as sacrificial offerings before the pyre of Patroclus (Il. 18:336–7; 23:22–23, 175–7). The "evil" (Greek *kaka*) character of Achilles' deed (Il. 23:176) does not mean that the poet condemns it; as shown by Od. 9:316, "evil" (*kaka*) can refer to fully justified vengeance. The appeasing of Patroclus' spirit by a group-sacrifice of foemen, is to be compared with David's group-sacrifice of Saul's descendants to appease the wronged Gibeonites (II Sam. 21.6–9). Both acts of brutality hail from the same heroic age in the East Mediterranean; and each is quite out of keeping with the classical Hebrew and Greek *mores* of later times. That the two acts are organically related

---

[96] Editors or scribes might alter or omit a strange feature that did not seem correct; but they would not spoil a clear text by injecting incomprehensible data.

in the epic repertoire is confirmed by specific detail. Rizpah lovingly guarded the victims' corpses, not allowing "the fowl of heaven to light upon them by day" nor "the beast of the field by night" (II Sam. 21.10); even as Aphrodite (Il. 23:185–6) kept the dogs from Hector's corpse by night and day.

123. The inevitability of death haunts man and his literature. That man can surmount his fear of death and prefer to live bravely rather than long, is not the monopoly of any one race or school of literature. The noble mood of the Iliad goes with a standard of values that places fame higher than longevity (e. g., Il. 9:412–6). In this regard the Iliad is anticipated by the Gilgamesh Epic (4:vi:39; 7:iii: 33 ff.), which sets a higher premium on fame than on life.

CHAPTER IV

Gods, Religion and Ritual

124. It is in the sphere of religion that our Greek and Hebrew texts are worlds apart (with Ugarit occupying an intermediate position). The Greco-Hebrew coincidences are numerous in detail (§§126–60) but the general picture is totally different in Homer and Bible. In Greek epic there is no emphasis on cult and the gods are humanized to a degree that makes them seem ludicrous to anyone steeped in a lofty concept of divinity. Devious politics, domestic brawls, sexual lust and the whole gamut of human frailties are attributed to the pantheon in a way that entertained the ancient listener but did not make him a devotee of, or strengthen his adherence to, any cult. In spite of the anthropomorphisms and anthropopathisms in the Old Testament, God is divine: distinct from, and above, man. Moreover, the narrative content of the Hebrew text is inseparably bound with the cult of Yahwe.

125. The gulf between Homeric and Biblical attitudes toward cult, results from the nature of their respective publics. Greek epic is addressed to the widely scattered Greek settlements, which may have known the same pantheon, but were quite varied as to cultic practice. To be effective in creating Greek nationhood, the Iliad could not take sides cultically. The Bible in general, and the Pentateuch in particular, did not aim at so large a public. Hebrew Scripture is addressed to the Children of Israel, united in the cult of Yahwe. (Had there been a Canaanite national epic, designed to embrace all the people of Canaan, the pantheon of Ṣāfôn, with El at the head, would have been portrayed much as the Olympians of Homer, under Zeus's leadership. But insistence on Baal's cult would have alienated Israel, even as insistence on Yahwism would have alienated the Phoenicians.)

126. Divinely fashioned staffs that secure victory are common in East Mediterranean myth and saga. Ugaritic text 68 tells how Baal vanquished Yamm by two magic clubs fashioned by Kothar-and-Hasis (§§141–2). But Greek and Hebrew legend share a special variety of divine staff constituting a close link between the two literatures. As long as Moses held up "the staff of God," the Children of Israel prevailed over their enemies, the Amalekites, till victory was won (Ex. 17.9–13). Lowering the staff had to be avoided lest the foe prevail (v. 11). Similarly, Phoebus Apollo (Il. 15:318–22) controls the tide of victory by the way he holds the aegis. And in Od. 22:297, Athene holds up the aegis so that her favorites may slay their foes. In other words, Moses' "staff of God" (cf. §156) is simply the Hebrew equivalent of what the Greeks term the *aigis*; both have the identical function of wondrous scepters used to secure victory.

127. Another striking parallel that transcends normal experience is the immobilizing of the sun in the heavens until an important mission is fulfilled. Hera does not permit the sun to set until Patroclus' corpse has been recovered (Il. 18:239–42). And in Il. 2:412–8, men pray that the sun may not set till victory has been won. This motif appears also in the Book of Jashar (Josh. 10.13–14), when the sun was stopped in its course until Israel won its battle.[97]

128. Job 26.7 states that God can suspend the earth on sheer nothingness. This probably means that God, to show his power, could remove the earth from the foundations on which

---

[97] Ugaritic *la šmm* (49:II:25; 51:VIII:22–23), "the heavens were fatigued, incapacitated" seems to refer to the stoppage of the sun, moon and stars.

it normally rests (Micah 6.2; etc.; Ug. 51:I:41) and hang it in space as Zeus threatens to do in Il. 8:26.

129. A nightmarish concept in the East Mediterranean was the thought of being swallowed alive into the underworld (Od. 12:21–22). Numbers 16 relates how the earth gaped and swallowed the wicked Korah, Datan and Abiram alive into Sheol (=Hades); cf. vv. 30–34. The Iliad (6:281–2; 8:150; cf. 17:416–7) also reflects the notion that the earth could gape and swallow reprehensible men.

130. The desire for immortality or eternal youth is almost universal. Both appear in the Gilgamesh Epic, where the hero in vain seeks immortality through deification; and though he finally obtains the magic plant that restores youth, he tragically loses it. East Mediterranean epic introduces a somewhat perverse version of this motif, with the result that it becomes less commonplace: a goddess offers immortality but the hero refuses it. Thus Calypso would make Odysseus deathless and ageless (Od. 23:336) but he refuses her offer, preferring to go home. Similarly, Anath offers eternal life to Aqhat in return for his bow, but he rejects her offer to his own hurt (2 Aqht:VI:26–30).

131. People have the gift of resolving contradictions without abandoning them. Gods are distinguished from men essentially through immortality. Yet Sarpedon, son of Zeus, did not escape death (see §44). As is often the case in such matters, our text of Homer injects a rational note, for Il. 24:258–9 states that Hector "*seemed* not the son of a mortal man, but of a god." The Epic of Kret (125:22–23) has a prince, confused by his father's pretensions to divinity, ask: "Can gods die? Yea, the scion of El not live?"

132. The epithet of Hades, "of the horses," (Il. 11:445) suggests a connection with Ugaritic texts 121–124, where the Rephaim (associated with the shades of the dead) are riders of horse-drawn chariots. This element looks Indo-European, for the earlier populations of the Near East did not use the horse. Thus while horses appear in Ugaritic epics (Kret and Aqhat), they do not appear in the more conservative myths of Ugarit, in which gods ride on donkey-back only.

133. The epic permits, and even delights in, the embarrassments to which a god may be subjected. Woes may be inflicted on gods by mortal men (Il. 5:382–404) and Jacob defeated a minor deity (Gen. 32.29).

134. Helius threatens Zeus that if the slaughter of his (Helius') sacred kine is not avenged, he will descend into Hades and shine among the dead (Od. 12:377–83); but Zeus wants the existing order preserved, with Helius shining on, among gods and men. Similarly, Ishtar threatens the head of the pantheon, her father Anu, as well as her mother Antum, that if she (Ishtar) is not allowed to take revenge on Gilgamesh, she will smash open the doors of the underworld and turn loose the dead to outnumber on earth the living (Gilgamesh Epic 6:80 ff.); cf. also the Descent of Ishtar:15–20. Anath threatens to make El's gray hair run with blood if he does not allow her to avenge herself on Aqhat (3 Aqht:rev. 11–12; cf. 'nt:V:32–33).

135. There is a cuneiform forerunner of Odysseus' threatening Circe with a sword so that she became terror stricken and offered him her love (Od. 10:321–35). In the Babylonian myth of Nergal and Ereshkigal, the goddess Ereshkigal, wishing to kill Nergal for an affront, summons him. He comes, but assuming the initiative, he seizes her by the hair and threatens to cut off her head, whereupon she proposes marriage. Nergal accepts, thus becoming the king of the underworld by marrying its queen.

136. Talking animals are common in fables but rare in the epic. The motif is not so preposterous as people unfamiliar with animals imagine. People who live with dogs, horses and other animals do commune with their beasts without words having to come from the beasts, nor for that matter from the people. In telling the story, however, it is necessary to transform the beasts' thoughts into words. To accept the transfer of human thoughts, while rejecting the transfer of animals' thoughts, into words, reflects not logic but unfamiliarity with animals. In the Late Egyptian Tale of the Two Brothers, Bata understands the language of the cows (which the text renders in plain Egyptian). The speech of Achilles' horse Xanthus (Il. 19:408–17) closely parallels that of Balaam's ass (Num. 22.28–30). In both cases, the human master has been unfair to the beast, whereupon the latter talks to its master "like a Dutch uncle." That Yahwe opened the mouth of the ass (Num. 22.28), as Hera gave speech to the horse (Il. 19:407), is a rationalizing touch, acknowledging that human speech is not natural for animals.

137. The theme of gods attending the wedding of a mortal appears in Il. 18:82–85; 24:62–63 (the marriage of Peleus) and in Ugaritic text 128:II (the marriage of Kret).

138. The highly polytheistic Near East had strong mono-theistic undercurrents that would come to the fore from time to time in widely separated areas. Ikhnaton's solar monotheistic revolution is the most spectacular example; Yahwism is histor-ically the most important.[98] Even in the crass polytheism of Homer, monotheistic notes are struck now and then. In Il. 21:103 (etc.), *theos* is not a "god" but the "God" (cf. Od. 14:444).

139. The assembly of the gods (Il. 8:2) where the deities confer is common throughout the Near East (and may be well nigh universal). In Ugarit the divine assembly is called *mpḫrt bn il* or *pḫr ilm* = Akkadian *puḫur ilâni*. The divine court also appears in Job 1.6 ff.; 2.1 ff. We are confronted with the projec-tion of human governmental institutions into the divine sphere.

140. The notion that a god (Poseidon) built the wide and fair wall of Troy (Il. 21:446–7) is anticipated in the Gilgamesh Epic (1:1 ff. = 11:end), according to which the Seven Wise Gods built the walls of Uruk.

141. Any two pantheons, even though they be historically unrelated, may have structural or typological resemblances of no significance in a study like this monograph. Any two pan-theons selected at random are likely to have a chief god with a chief wife, and to have one or more deities concerned with fertility. However, in the East Mediterranean, the impact of Crete was so strong artistically, that the god of arts and crafts in any pantheon of the area is likely to be essentially a reflex of a Cretan prototype. Ugarit represents its artisan god Kothar-and-Hasis as Caphtorian, in the Idaean tradition (§38). That the Ida of craftsmanship is not Anatolian (such as the Ida over-looking Troy) but Cretan, is indicated by Pliny (Natural History

[98] See *Journal of Near Eastern Studies* 13, 1954, pp. 56–59.

7:56, 197): . . . *Ferrum conflare et temperare Hesiodus in Creta eos (monstrasse) qui vocati sunt Dactyli Idaei*; i. e., Hesiod states that the Idaean Dactyls taught the smelting and tempering of iron in Crete. In any event, the Greek account of Hephaistus has much in common with the Ugaritic picture of Kothar-and-Hasis, in general and in detail.

142. Hephaistus' bellows (Il. 18:409, 412, 470) and tongs (:477) are matched by Kothar-and-Hasis' bellows and tongs (51:I:24-25). Hephaistus (Il. 1:606-8; 14:166-8) is the builder of palaces for the gods exactly like Kothar-and-Hasis (51:I-VI). Hephaistus' famed fire (Il. 2:426; 9:468; 23:33) is to be compared with Kothar-and-Hasis' stupendous fire which burns for a week, culminating in the completion of Baal's palace (51:VI: 22-33).

143. Baal invited a number of deities to his housewarming including bovine gods and goddesses and jar gods and goddesses (51:VI:49-54). The concepts underlying this incident were common in the East Mediterranean. Od. 12:131 shows that the kine of Helius were immortal, which is tantamount to divine. And Il. 18:373-7 tells how Hephaistus made tripods with golden wheels, so that they enter automatically the gathering of the gods and thereafter go home again. Wheeled tripods have been found in Greece, and tripods were used at Ugarit. The fact that Hephaistus animated the tripods so that they could on their own initiative go to and from the assembly of the gods, shows that they were members of the pantheon to be compared with the jar gods and goddesses of the Ugaritic pantheon attending Baal's feast. Perhaps the best translation for those Ugaritic jar deities is "deified tripods."

144. Hephaistus' wondrous skill produced also golden effigies of girls that he animated to act alive and serve him (Il. 18:416-20). This too has a Ugaritic parallel, for El animates two effigies that become his wives (text 52).

145. The artisan god supplies the means of vanquishing a water deity in both Ugaritic and Homeric literature. Kothar-and-Hasis equips Baal with the weapons for defeating the sea god Yamm (text 68; cf. §126). Achilles is rescued from the river

60

that the gods called Xanthus, but men call Scamander,[99] by means of Hephaistus' weapon, fire (Il. 20:73-74; 21:331-60). For fire devouring the Great Deep, see also Amos 7.4.

146. The name Kothar-and-Hasis is of the "A-and-B" type, which is common among the names of deities in the Ugaritic pantheon (*Ugaritic Manual* §8.54). This type of name occurs also in Greek; e. g., the god *Kratos-Bia-te*, "Power-and-Force" (Aeschylus, *Prometheus Bound* :12).

147. In §145 it was pointed out that the river had two names: Xanthus or Scamander. Optional names recur often enough in Homer; e. g., Paris = Alexander or Scamandrius = Astyanax (Il. 6:402-3).[100] In Ugarit, Baal = Hadd. In the Bible, Reuel = Jethro, Jacob = Israel, Solomon = Jedediah, etc. The origin of these double names need not be the same typologically in every instance. We are not endeavoring to reduce all the illustrations to a single formula. But we can assert with confidence that double names are so common that they cannot be regarded as criteria for detaching literary strata in accordance with a documentary hypothesis.

148. Athene (Il. 8:389), like Elijah (II Kings 2.11) is borne by a fiery chariot. Such analogues suggest that the Tales of the Prophets (as distinct from the annalistic sources of Kings) draw on epic tradition (without necessarily implying a poetic *Vorlage* of those Tales). This suggestion is supported by other evidence. In I Kings 18, Elijah brings down fire upon his altar by praying to God. This may be compared with Il. 23:192 telling that the pyre of Patroclus would not kindle; but then, in response to Achilles' prayer (:193-8, 205-11), Iris got the North and West wind gods to set the fire. I Chron. 21.26 deals with the same

[99] Double nomenclature, in the respective languages of men and of gods, appears in Sanskrit, Hittite, Greek and Icelandic literatures pointing to an Indo-European origin of the phenomenon in the East Mediterranean. For sample passages, see J. Friedrich, "Göttersprache und Menschensprache im hethitischen Schrifttum," *Sprachgeschichte und Wortbedeutung, Festschrift Albert Debrunner*, 1954, pp. 135-9.

[100] Double naming in Homer is treated comprehensively by L. Ph. Rank, *Etymologiseering en verwante Verschijnselen bij Homerus*, Assen, 1951, pp. 109-29.

motif; David called to God who in response sent down fire to consume the sacrifice. As is often the case, Chronicles preserves old material not to be found in the parallel sections of Samuel and Kings. In this instance, the material must stem from older epic sources; it cannot be a late invention of the Chronicler, who lived in Achaemenian times, when the spirit of the East Mediterranean epic age was long past.

149. The divine promise that the hero's line will continue is a basic theme handled quite similarly in both Ugaritic epic and Patriarchal Narratives. In the Epics of Kret and Aqhat, the birth of the male heir is a major motif. Lest we misconstrue this as universal, it might be well to point out that from Genesis through Kings, the theme persists down to the birth of Samuel, never to recur in Old Testament history. It must have remained a frequent feature in real life, but it was no longer considered worthy of saga. It is absent from the long history of the United and Divided Monarchies.[101]

150. This theme is found among the ancient Greeks with the result that we must consider it East Mediterranean, rather than just Canaanite. In the Homeric Hymn to Aphrodite (:196-7), the goddess promises an eternal line to Anchises, and she names his son Aeneas because she "felt awful (*ainos*) grief" (:198-9). This is of a piece with the divine promise to Abram that he would become a nation (Gen. 12.2) through his progeny.

151. The etymologizing of names such as "Aeneas" (§150) is common among the Greeks. Note also Od. 1:62 where "Odysseus" is derived from *odyssomai*, "I grieve." This habit continued among Greek authors including the most sober historians. Such etymologizing (usually of an etiological character) permeates Hebrew tradition too; e. g., the etymology of "Noah" in Gen. 5.29; etc., etc.

152. In Ugarit, the sea god Yamm was an older deity from whom the more youthful Baal wrested dominion (text 68). In Od. 4:399-463 we read of how Menelaus overpowered Proteus, the old god of the sea. It is risky to strain the common elements in two stories with considerable differences: one being in the

---

[101] See my article "The Patriarchal Age," *Journal of Bible and Religion* 21, 1953, pp. 238-43.

realm of divine mythology, the other in the epic repertoire of heroic men. Moreover, sea-yarns are common wherever men sail the seas. Yet it stands to reason that a culture whose unifying channel was a sea, would probably possess some notions of the sea spread over the general area. Striking is the parallel to the Greek "backward-flowing Ocean" (Hesiod, Theogony:776; Il. 18:399) in the Psalms (114.3): "The Sea looked and fled; the Jordan turned backwards." Be it noted that Ocean/Sea is often classified as, and stands parallel to, "river" in Greek (Il. 20:7) as well as Hebrew poetry. Yamm is "Ruler/Judge River" in Ugaritic. Canaanite Yamm (or Greek "Ocean") may be regarded as the King of Rivers. The judicial meaning of "judge" is also present; for court ordeals were often made in a river;[102] cf. the Styx as "the dread river of oath" (Il. 2:755).

153. Because anthropopathism is so common, it is impossible to separate divine wrath from human wrath (§92) as an epic theme. Achilles' wrath (Il. 19:367) is a prelude to his victory; Patroclus' heart is full of wrath as he wages his heroic battle (Il. 16:585); Odysseus, wroth for his comrade's sake, fights furiously and well (Il. 4:501). In this, the divine matches the human; cf. Achilles' wrath against the Trojans (Il. 19:367) with Hera's wrath against the Trojans (Il. 18:367). Other examples of divine wrath are found in Il. 4:166–8; 5:178, 191; 15:72; *et passim.*

154. In the Song of the Sea, one of the untransformed fragments of Hebrew epic, Yahwe is called a "man of war" (Ex. 15.3), whose "wrath" (:7) consumes the enemy as fire burns stubble. This passage leaves no doubt that in Yahwe, the wrath of God and of the warrior, is one and the same. A book, many times the size of this monograph, could and should be written about the Bible theme of the wrath of God against the background of East Mediterranean epic.

155. The subsidence of anger is a favorite theme in East Mediterranean literature. Achilles' reconciliation with Agamemnon (Il. 19:35, 56–75) precedes the favorable turn in the war. Moreover the once wrathful Achilles relents in the presence of the suppliant Priam, to whom he grants the body of Hector.

---

[102] *E. g.*, in Hammurabi's Code, §§2, 132.

The Bible often represents God as at first wrathful but later relenting. An angry God destroys the world by flood, only to relent and promise the survivors that he will never again visit such a punishment on this imperfect world. This motif continues to re-echo throughout Scripture. A particularly fine example is the Book of Jonah, in which God, resolved on destroying Nineveh, countenances the contrition of the wicked city and forgivingly spares it. Note also the storm at sea, manifesting divine wrath, that also subsides (Jonah 1.15). Jonah's (2.4) being encompassed by "River" may reflect the same theme that appears in Achilles' fight with the River Xanthus. When Il. 24:8 tells of "the wars of men and the grievous waves," we are reminded of Jonah's (2.4) battle with the waves. As Jonah (2.2–10) prays for salvation from the personified Deep (v. 6), Odysseus prays to the river god to save him from Poseidon (Od. 5:445–54). These parallels between Jonah and Homer may seem too general to count for much. Accordingly, a more striking parallel is called for: Just as Jonah (4.6) rejoices over the plant that shaded him, so does Odysseus (Od. 5:474–487; N. B.: line 486) rejoice over the thorn bush and olive that protect him from the elements.

156. The epic fluidity between men and gods is familiar to any reader of Homer. But that this once characterized the early Hebraic traditions has been obscured by the monotheistic filter through which the *textus receptus* has passed. Yet enough tell-tale evidence has survived so that no doubt remains as to the general picture. The mating of deities with the daughters of men to sire the famous heroes of old (Gen. 6.4) is unequivocal. Nor can the assumption of Enoch (Gen. 5.24) imply anything less than apotheosis. Ex. 7.1 states that Yahwe upgraded Moses to a deity in preparation for the mission of Moses with Pharaoh.

157. That gods and men should have dealings with one another is universal. It is only when they are involved in a highly specific situation that such dealings are meaningful for our investigation. Such a situation appears in Homer; to wit, an enraged hero, about to use his sword indiscreetly, is withheld from committing violence by a pair of goddesses. In Il. 1:188 ff., Athene, sent by Hera, stops Achilles who was drawing his sword to kill Agamemnon. Achilles decides to obey the two of them

(:216); i. e., Hera and Athene. In much the same situation, Astarte and Anath grab the hands of Baal and prevent him from stabbing the emissaries of the sea-god Yamm (Ug. text 137:38 ff.).

158. Gods have it in their power to impart to mortals a glow of glory. For instance, Athene (Il. 5:1–8) kindled the head and shoulders of Diomedes with light. Cf. also Od. 18:354–5 for the divine glare from Odysseus' head (although the theme is turned into a jest). This motif (which has a counterpart in the artistic tradition of the halo) is reflected in the glorification of Moses, who came down from Mount Sinai with the skin of his face gleaming (Ex. 34.29, 30, 35).

159. Athene also glorifies her favorites by making them taller and comelier; thus Laertes (Od. 24:367–9), Penelope (Od. 18:192–6, 248–9) and Odysseus (Od. 6:227–31; 23:156–8). When I Sam. 10.23 states that Saul "was higher than all the people, from his shoulders and upwards" when he became king, it may be that we are dealing with a toned-down glorification that originally had Saul made taller on the occasion by divine grace.[103]

160. The account of Moses is full of East Mediterranean elements (§40). We have already noted his deification in Ex. 7.1 (§156). The statements in Deut. 34.6, 7 that his grave is unknown and that he never lost his vigor may substitute an earlier (or, at least, another) version attributing to him outright apotheosis. The pseudepigraphical Assumption of Moses[104] may preserve the kernel of an old tradition, now expunged from our Biblical text in accordance with monotheistic scruples. Ex. 34.29, 30, 35 inform us that Moses' face beamed with the light of divine glorification when he descended from Mount Sinai. Cf. Il. 18:225–7, which tells that Athene glorified Achilles with fire blazing around his head. Moreover, just as Aaron and the Children of Israel were frightened upon seeing Moses in his glorified state (Ex. 34:30), Telemachus was frightened (Od. 16:178–85) upon seeing Odysseus glorified in appearance by Athene and therefore looking like a god.

[103] In which case, I Sam. 9.2 would be anticipatory.
[104] See R. H. Charles, *The Apocrypha and Pseudepigrapha of the Old Testament*, Oxford, 1913.

161. The people's complaints against Moses may prove to be an epic feature of a piece with the people's complaints against Agamemnon. Rebelliousness over which the leader must triumph seems to be one of the themes favored in the epic repertoire. In Ugaritic, Prince Yṣb rebels against his father, King Kret; in the Bible, Absalom rebels against his father King David. This in no way calls into question the historicity of Absalom's revolt. We seek rather to explain the prominence given to it on the ground that the epic repertoire called for highlighting the rebellion of a prince against his kingly father.

CHAPTER V

STYLE AND IDIOM

162. Stylistically, many points of contact between Homer and Bible are bridged by Ugarit. The epic clichés provide clear illustrations; e. g., in Ugaritic, direct discourse is often introduced by "he lifted his voice and shouted." The same type of parallelistic cliché appears in Homeric "but Hector lifted his voice and cried aloud to the Trojans" (Il. 6:110) or "he lifted his voice and called in piercing cry to the Danaans" (Il. 11:275, 585). Cf. the Hebrew "and Job answered and said" (Job 12.1; 16.1; etc.), "and he lifted his parable and said" (Num. 23.18; 24:3), "and he lifted his voice and wept" (Gen. 29.11).[105]

163. In relating the dispatch of messengers, it was customary to say that they not only heard or obeyed, but also that they did not disregard their orders. Thus the fulfilment of the command is stated first positively and then negatively, hand in hand with parallelistic form. The Ugaritic formula is "the messengers departed; they did not sit."[106] Cf. "he spoke, and the herald heard and did not disobey him" (Il. 4:198). For the negative manner, note also "he spoke and swift wind-footed Iris did not disobey him" (Il. 11:195; etc.).

[105] The stylistic relations between Ugaritic and Hebrew literatures are well illustrated by U. Cassuto, *The Goddess Anath* [in Hebrew], Jerusalem, 1951, pp. 19–41; also 2nd. ed., 1953.
[106] *E. g.*, Krt: 300–1.

164. A culture whose hub is the sea must necessarily have a common nautical heritage in its literature. Iris is described as speeding down into the depths of the sea like a plummet of lead (Il. 24:80). Cf. Ex. 15.10 which states that the Egyptian foemen "sank like lead into great waters." The figure arose from the use of lead plummets for sounding depths.

165. A detailed study of shifts from person to person in discourse, would be of interest. In Ex. 23.25 there is a shift from third to first person, tantamount to a change from narration to quotation. In Il. 16:5–6 the third person shifts in line 20 to second person; similarly in Il. 16:584.

166. The gulf between dactylic hexameter and Semitic parallelism is great. Ancient Ugaritic, Hebrew and other Semitic poetry has no regular meter in the sense that Greek epic possesses it. The essence of Semitic poetic form is parallelism, whereby stichoi balance each other in thought. Parallel members tend to approximate each other in length; for the use of ballast variants in the second stichos[107] to compensate for the omission of an element present in the first stichos, shows that bulk-balance was sought as a corollary of sense-balance. But bulk-balance is not the same as meter whereby the line can have only so many feet, which in turn must conform to a pattern with a narrow and exactly definable margin of variation.[108]

167. Meter would not be objected to, in Semitic poetry; just as parallelism is not ruled out in Greek epic. But such meter (in Hebrew) and parallelism (in Greek) are then optional and occasional features; they are not essential. This means that just as it is unjustified to emend a Homeric line to make it parallelistic, it is unjustified to emend a Hebrew verse *metri causa*.[109]

[107] For a detailed analysis of Ugaritic poetic structure, see *Ugaritic Manual* §13.99–161; for ballast variants, note §13.107.

[108] The attempts to establish meter for ancient Semitic poetry hinge on a vague definition of meter, or require arbitrary emendations of the texts (including cuneiform originals) to fit the hypothetical system. One of the strange points of view is that Semitic has "mixed meter." Obviously, a mixture which cannot be reduced to any formulation is quite the opposite of metric principle.

[109] A glance at the table of symbols and a study of the critical notes in the Kittel Hebrew Bible will show to what extent *metri causa* alterations are proposed by the leaders of textual criticism.

168. And yet, in spite of the gulf that divides Greek from Semitic poetic form, there are links resulting from a common heritage. The sharp break in the middle of each Hebrew or Ugaritic verse, is the inescapable consequence of parallelism. In dactylic hexameter, the cesura in the middle of the line has no function that seems formally necessary; and accordingly it may reflect the influence of parallelism in the pre-Homeric East Mediterranean.

169. All through the Near East (and doubtless also beyond it), persons may be said to be clothed in such and such a characteristic. Il. 9:372 speaks of one clothed in shamelessness. We need, for present purposes, call attention only to a specific characteristic treated in this fashion in both Homer and Bible; to wit, Od. 9:214 mentions one "clothed in great might"; similarly "if you do not clothe yourself in might" (Il. 9:231). Compare Ps. 93.1 where Yahwe is clothed in might. The symbolism of wearing certain abstract qualities appears also in magic literature, such as the Uruk incantation, in which a formula states that the patient is stript of his garb of rage and clad with the garb of well-being.[110]

170. Common background has evoked the use of specific similes shared by various branches of East Mediterranean literature. For example, the form of a maiden may be likened to a stately palm tree. Od. 6:163 compares Nausicaa to a palm. Canticles 7.8 likens the form of the girl to a palm, adding that her breasts are like clusters of grapes. The combination of grape and palm results from the fact that the vines were trained on palms instead of on trellises. Palm groves with clusters of grapes hanging from the palm branches are portrayed on Assyrian reliefs.

171. Comparing a fleet-footed youth to a deer must be all but universal. Yet the prominence given to it in East Mediterranean literature is of interest. In David's dirge (II Sam. 1.19) heroes are called "deer." Joab's brother Asahel is said to have been fleet of foot like a deer in the fields (II Sam. 2.18). One of the honorific titles of heroes in Ugaritic is "deer" (*Ug. Manual*

---

[110] Transliterated and translated in *Orientalia* 9, 1940, pp. 29–38.

§20.772). The Greeks, unlike the Semites, were fond of the
dog and used it in hunting.[111] Accordingly, while the hero Hector
is compared with a deer, Achilles, who overtook and vanquished
him, is likened to a hound (Il. 22:189–190).

172. Homer often uses "dalliance" to refer not to sex but to
war (Il. 11:502; 13:291, 779; 17:228; 22:126–8). The application
of a word for "dalliance" to "fighting" has a parallel in Hebrew.
The root *ṣḥq* (lit., "to laugh") has the meaning "to play with,"
including sexual dalliance; cf. Isaac's dalliance with his wife
Rebecca in Gen. 26.8. This very word refers to the deadliest
kind of combat in II Sam. 2.14 where "Abner said to Joab: 'Let
the youths arise and play (*sic!*) before us.' " The "play" resulted
in the death of all the contestants (v. 16).

173. Pairs of antonyms to designate totality are common all
over the world. We say "they came great and small" to signify
"everybody came." But certain specific pairs are not universal.
For example, the "tree of knowledge, good and evil"[112] means
simply the "tree of all kinds of knowledge," though the fact
that "good and evil" does not occur as a universalism in English
hides the plain sense of the passage from the English reader. Od.
4:392 uses "evil and good" in the sense of "everything"; cf. "all
things, good and evil" (Od. 20:85–86; cf. :309–10) and "I know
each thing, the good and the evil" (Od. 18:228–9).

174. The hero's apology for his past conduct is included in
the repertoire. Achilles' apology (Il. 9:308 ff., 320 ff.) is to be
compared with Jacob's (Gen. 31); both are in direct discourse.

175. The sympathetic presentation of the *dramatis personae*
opposed to the heroes appears in Od. 2:85–128, where the wooers'
side is favorably portrayed against the wily Penelope. Cf. Gen.
31, in which Laban's side of the story is given, as well as Jacob's,
even though the sympathies of the author are squarely with
the guileful Jacob. The favorable light in which the Trojans are

[111] Ugaritic literature, while couched in Semitic, occupies an intermediate
position socially. Thus dogs, in the Epic of Kret, are at home in the palaces
of kings, quite as in the Homeric epics. Nor are swine taboo in Ugarit.

[112] This point and its implications (*cf.* Gen. 2.17; 3.22) are discussed in
Introduction to Old Testament Times, pp. 22–23. For "good + evil = totality,"
see also Gen. 24.50; I Sam. 22.15; I Kings 3.7; Zeph. 1.12; Prov. 15.3.

shown in the Iliad, does not come under this heading. The Trojans are no less heroic than the Achaeans, once we understand the function of the Iliad (§23). While the Od. and Gen. passages just cited might possibly be due to a natural sympathy for the victims of guile, they might also be a legacy from national epic, in which both sides must be treated kindly in order to fulfil the purpose of welding them together.

176. Instructions not to tell a lady unpleasant news lest it upset her, appear in Od. 2:372-6, where Telemachus leaves instructions not to inform Penelope of his departure lest she mar her fair flesh with weeping. Similarly, the sick Kret tells his son Ilhu not to tell Octavia that he, Kret, is ill, because she is tenderhearted and will be distressed (125:31 ff.).

177. The epithet "single-hoofed" (applied to horses in Il. 5:236, 321; 19:end) brings up an interesting point. Most people are not concerned with whether their animals are single or cloven hoofed. But East Mediterranean usage did make an issue of it. This happens to be a cornerstone of the Mosaic classification of quadrupeds. To be ritually edible a quadruped has to be cloven hoofed as well as ruminating. The Hebrew abhorrence of swine may also have some precedent in the East Mediterranean. The transformation of Odysseus' comrades by Circe may be the more tragic, because, of all beasts, they were turned into swine.

178. The climaxing of "3" by "4" is frequent in Homer (Od. 2:89, 107; cf. *Rivista degli Studi Orientali* 29, 1954, pp. 167-8). This is well attested in the Bible too; e. g., (Amos 1.3, 6, 9, 11, 13; 2.1, 4, 6) "for the 3 sins of N; yea for 4, I would not reverse it"; cf. Prov. 30.15, 18, 21, 29.

179. The climaxing of "6 days" by "the 7th" is so frequent in Homer, Ugarit and the Bible (*Rivista degli Studi Orientali* 29, 1954, pp. 168-9), that the seven day week, whereby the six working days are climaxed by the Sabbath, can only go back to pre-Mosaic East Mediterranean usage. This usage may have reached the area from Mesopotamia for the climaxing of 6 days by the 7th is familiar, for example, in the Gilgamesh Epic; e. g., 11:127-30, where the 6 days of the flood-storm is climaxed by calm on the 7th; and 11:142-6, where after the ark

70

remains motionless on the mountain for 6 days, Utnapishtim sends forth the dove on the 7th.

180. The 7-day grouping triumphed over competition from other groupings. The 9-day period is attested in Homer (e. g., Il. 6:174) and Egyptian (e. g., in the Wenamon text, a guest spends 9 days with his host in accordance with a literary cliché).

181. The climaxing of "12" by "13" (see Il. 10:488 ‖ 495 and 560 ‖ 561), where an examination of the context shows that the higher number is logically "14", has a striking parallel in Gen. 14.4–5 where the series "12 ‖ 13 ‖ 14" occurs. The fact that Gen. 14 is atypical in the Patriarchal Narratives and that "12 ‖ 13 ‖ 14" is unique in the Old Testament, suggests that Gen. 14 and Il. 10:488, 495, 560–1 share a common (Indo-European?) influence that penetrated the East Mediterranean.

182. The number "20" enjoys a special status (§78). Note Od. 5:34 where an arrival on the 20th day is reported. Menelaus and Helen are separated for 20 years; so are Odysseus and Penelope. Gen. 31.38 gives Jacob's sojourn with Laban as of 20 years duration. In the Book of Judges there are examples of time-reckoning in multiples of 20; thus 20 years (4:3), 40 years (5:31) and 80 years (3:30).

183. In Ugaritic (52:67; 75:II:46), "years" may be paralleled by a synonym meaning "circling ones." The Homeric reflexes of this synonym are used adjectivally; e. g., "in ten circling years" (Il. 8:404, 418), "in five circling years" (Il. 23:833).

SUMMARY

184. The meeting of many peoples in the Levant during the second millennium B. C. converted the East Mediterranean into the focal point of world history and produced the synthesis that gave birth to Western Civilization. The peoples involved were varied. Some contributed the heritage of Mesopotamia and Egypt. At the center were the Minoans who stimulated their less developed neighbors such as the Greeks and Hebrews to produce civilizations of their own.

185. We are often able to identify Sumero-Akkadian, Hittite, and Egyptian contributions to East Mediterranean literature by

the help of cuneiform and Egyptian texts. Much must have been contributed by the Greeks and other Indo-European nations — to say nothing of the many other known ethnic factors — but it is idle for us to disseminate speculation when so much solid work can be done.

186. Geography and archeology have long indicated that the Greeks and Hebrews started on their historic careers in different but interrelated segments of the East Mediterranean. Bold spirits have intermittently maintained the kinship of early Greece and the ancient Near East. Now Ugarit at last provides the literary link connecting Israel and Hellas.

187. No longer can we assume that Greece is the hermetically sealed Olympian miracle, any more than we can consider Israel the vacuum-packed miracle from Sinai. Rather must we view Greek and Hebrew civilizations as parallel structures built upon the same East Mediterranean foundation.